RAPTURE

AND

REVELATION:

Welcome to the End Time

RAPTURE

AND

REVELATION:

Welcome to the End Time

LYNN BABER

Rapture and Revelation

Edited by Barbara Schoeneberger

Published by Ark Press 2012
PO Box 1436
Weatherford, TX 76086

ISBN 978-1-938836-02-2

INSPIRATION

"Therefore, if anyone is in Christ, he is a new creation; old things have passed away; behold, all things have become new."

2 Corinthians 5:17

"These things I have spoken to you, that in Me you may have peace. In the world you will have tribulation; but be of good cheer, I have overcome the world."

John 16:33

Table of Contents

Introduction

"Now this I say, brethren, that flesh and blood cannot inherit the kingdom of God; nor does corruption inherit incorruption. Behold, I tell you a mystery: We shall not all sleep, but we shall all be changed— "- 1 Corinthians 15:50-51

Welcome to the End Time.

Rapture and Revelation will not tell you what to believe, but it will ask you to be honest about *why* you believe *what* you do. This old world is rapidly aging as fires, floods, droughts, earthquakes, and storms ravage every continent. The clock of human history is quickly running down as nations, economies, and religions are either at war with one another or ready to implode upon themselves.

There is an absolute need for messages that offer the simple truth about the times we live in. Trust is something you remember from the good old days, not something you can teach your children today by pointing out a politician, doctor, news anchor, minister, or teacher. Watch the news long enough and you'll have ample reason to distrust all of the above. The absence of trust is the beginning of fear.

False teaching is the greatest hazard for today's Christians. How do you know that many of your core beliefs are not the result of false teaching that originated in false prophecy? *Rapture and Revelation* will challenge you to examine what you believe and compare it to the source - God's Word.

"Beloved, do not believe every spirit, but test the spirits, whether they are of God; because many false prophets have gone out into the world. And this is the spirit of the Antichrist, which you have heard was coming, and is now already in the world." - 1 John 4:1, 3

One choice eclipses all others, the choice between God and Not God. Sure, it sounds like an easy choice and every Christian would probably say, "Of course I choose God." Unfortunately, many of them would be wrong.

Our society is divided on almost every topic from ecology to abortion. If there was one thing most people might agree upon it would be that there is no such thing as absolute truth. Do you believe that anything is absolutely true or right in all instances and circumstances without exception? What would that be?

Do you believe that the Bible is the inerrant and inspired Word of God and that every single verse is true? Are you sure you know what I mean by 'Bible'? Whether or not you participate in the Rapture may depend upon knowing the difference between what five familiar words used to mean and what they mean today.

These five words no longer have a common definition which makes speaking or debating issues of politics, culture, or faith a real mess. In fact, it isn't even possible to define these words unless you first resolve the issue of whether or not absolutes exist.

- God
- Jesus
- Christian
- Grace
- Antichrist

There are as many unique relationships with God as there are humans. Just as every parent-child relationship is different so is the experience of every child of the King of Kings who pursues right relationship with Him. The experience of any friend, pastor, teacher, or writer will not be the same as yours. Yours will not be the same as mine. We are children of the same true God but no two will ever walk an identical path of sanctification. *Rapture and Revelation* is a tool for your use, intended to enlighten and support you as you persevere with all in the family of Christ.

Are you sure you know *why* you believe *what* you believe?

Are you certain you define God the same way your friends do? Are the lessons about tolerance and spirituality taught in public schools consistent with God's Word or some other gospel that has nothing to do with Jesus of Nazareth? Does your pastor preach the words of the apostles or those approved by a more progressive theology? If you don't know exactly how simple words like Jesus, Christian, and Grace are used, how will you know if what you hear is true or false?

"Not everyone who says to Me, 'Lord, Lord,' shall enter the kingdom of heaven, but he who does the will of My Father in heaven. Many will say to Me in that day, 'Lord, Lord, have we not prophesied in Your name, cast out demons in Your name, and done many wonders in Your name?' And then I will declare to them, 'I never knew you; depart from Me, you who practice lawlessness!' "
- Matthew 7:21-24

How can you be certain that the Jesus you know is the one who needs to know you? Of course, some popular Christian denominations would assure you it doesn't really matter and that all will be well. They're wrong.

Bible scholarship is simply that -- the study of a book titled The Bible. Every academic who studies the words in that book is free to teach whatever opinion he or she draws from the exercise - and they do. The best, brightest, and most credentialed academics across twenty centuries do not agree on what the Bible says. I'm not suggesting I belong among those scholars. I'm just a regular person tapped by God to serve the family of Christ. The ultimate responsibility to "rightly divide" the Word of God is yours alone. [2 Timothy 2:15]

This is the End Time. Perhaps you will see Jesus Christ today. But even if the Rapture does not occur in your natural lifetime, living in harmony, peace, and joy with God will bless you every day until you finally pass into immortality.

How do I know this is the End Time? The morning of March 11, 2011 changed my life forever.

Welcome to the End Time

"And you will hear of wars and rumors of wars. See that you are not troubled; for all these things must come to pass, but the end is not yet. For nation will rise against nation, and kingdom against kingdom. And there will be famines, pestilences, and earthquakes in various places. All these are the beginning of sorrows."
- Matthew 24:6-8.

"Tell them."

As I crossed the border from dreamland to awareness on what would normally have been a gorgeous spring day in north central Texas those were the words I "heard" in my head.

"Tell them."

The high for the day would be a balmy 77 degrees. The previous night's cool low of 46 degrees made the light cover on our bed feel delightfully cozy. The first audible words I heard that morning were, "Did you hear the news about the earthquake in Japan?" My husband had wakened extra early to watch the news while I continued to dream about the escapades of a rambunctious foal.

Once the dream fog cleared my first thought was, "The King is coming." It was the morning of March 11, 2011; the day that signaled the beginning of the End Time for me.

Two years ago I was a semi-retired horse professional turned writer and began working exclusively for God. I believe He asked me to write because it's not something I did. My choice would have been to work for Him from horseback but it seemed He had other ideas.

[13]

Usually books written about Revelation, Rapture, and the End Time can be a bit intimidating; combining esoteric scholarship, exegesis, and eschatology into one bound work of complexity as the author attempts to teach or sway the reader.

Okay, that was the end of the really big words.

What you'll find in this book is not miraculous or complex. It does not speculate about the date for either the Rapture or the second coming of Christ. The purpose of *Rapture and Revelation* is to offer three simple messages:

1. The King is coming.
2. This is the End Time.
3. You must choose now - God or Not God.

No one is going to knock on your door and prove to you that this is the moment for decision. No one is going to make you pay attention to the mounting evidence that the end of the world as we know it is near. The only thing that will save you is the quality of your relationship with Jesus. Relationships are personal; it's just you and Him.

The "One Thing"

Remember the movie *Cityslickers*? Billy Crystal's character, Mitch, was painfully intimidated by Curly (Jack Palance). At one point tough-and-gruff Curly asked the quivering Mitch this question:

Curly: Do you know what the secret of life is? *[holds up one finger]* This.
Mitch: Your finger?
Curly: One thing. Just one thing. You stick to that and the rest don't mean s***.
Mitch: But, what is the "one thing?"
Curly: That's what you have to find out.

[14]

The "one thing" for Christians is the Word of God. The word is the Bible and the Word is the person of Jesus Christ. That's it. Every Christian consideration, conclusion, and decision must be based on who Jesus is and what He asks of us.

If you have more than one child or have a brother or sister, you know that each parent-child relationship is different from every other. The same is true of the relationship each child of the King enjoys with his or her heavenly Father.

There is only one thing, but the particulars of that one thing differ from one Christian to another. There are scriptures that may be rightly understood in more than one way. Paul tells us not to argue over disputable things, but the foundational truth of the Word forms immovable bedrock that permits no wiggle room.

There is only one Way. There is only one God. There is only one source of truth. There is only one body of Christ, and there is only one brand of Christianity.

Pastors, politicians, authors, scholars and teachers will tell you there is more than one way to eternal life, there is more to the concept of *god* than what the Bible speaks, that truth is relative and that "my truth" may not be the same as "your truth."

There is diversity within the body of Christ. There is diversity between the relationship one child has with the Lord and another's. But there is no diversity of truth. Any teaching that truth is relative is a lie.

I was a horse trainer for a long time and learned the value of simplicity. I didn't write this book to get grant money, as a thesis for seminary or college, or to establish myself as an authority. If you've read one of my other books you know that animals, particularly horses and dogs, play a huge part of my story. So why did I write a book on Rapture and Revelation? The short answer is that I was instructed to write it. I realize that isn't reason enough for you to read it, so let me share just a bit more.

Some of the people I interact with regularly are depressed, disillusioned, or in despair. Jesus did not leave us without hope when He ascended to heaven. He left us with a peace and joy that are eternal and unshakeable. Rumbles of war, earthquakes, economic failure, drought, and flood are not big enough to negate the promises He made. Children of God have no reason for fear, and embracing fear is highly disrespectful to our Lord.

There are only two reasons a Christian experiences fear:

1. Doubt that God is able to handle the situation.
2. Doubt that God will handle it the way you want Him to.

There are serious choices that must be made and every choice you make matters. We are in the End Time. You may not have the opportunity to change your mind tomorrow if you make the wrong decision today. Any concept of living for tomorrow needs to be thrown out like yesterday's trash.

Looking to the Heavens

Christians have been looking to the heavens for some sign announcing Rapture since the day after Jesus ascended to His Father. Each of us yearns for our eternal home and we strain to find the way. With increasing frequency I hear folks say they believe Christ will be coming soon and they can't wait for the day. Many are tired of fighting the decline of the world, the decay of their bodies - or both.

Apostle Paul was no different from those who search the heavens today. Paul expressed his conflict between the call of his ministry

[16]

and the desire to be "out of here" in 2 Corinthians 5:1-9. He was intimately acquainted with physical suffering and personal persecution. Imagine the pain and scars from the abuse he suffered throughout his ministry. In the first century there were no corner drug stores selling pain medications, arthritis creams, or antibiotics. Paul groaned in his earthly tent - his failing mortal body - and earnestly desired the immortal body promised to each of us when we pass from this plane to the next.

Few mature Christians actually fear death -- at least that's what they say. What causes concern for many is the process of dying. That concern stems from contemplating the circumstances that might precede that last breath before your spirit escapes the surly bonds of earth and is free to occupy a new body and a new residence in eternity.

Yet Family members continue to search the heavens, desiring to be lifted from the world to meet Jesus in the air. While we remain in our bodies we are "absent from the Lord." We don't just understand Paul's conflict -- we own it. Are you ready to be gone but not quite sure you're ready to make the journey? Isn't avoiding the process of death one reason to hope for an imminent Rapture? Being lifted supernaturally into the air sounds a lot less painful than Alzheimer's, terminal cancer, or suffering an extended debilitating illness.

Whether the Rapture comes tomorrow or 500 years from now, you must be ready. The train is approaching and you must be on the platform prepared to board. The Bridegroom is coming.

Welcome to the End Time

"But where are thy gods that thou hast made thee? Let them arise, if they can save thee in the time of thy trouble:" - Jeremiah 2:28

The End Time is here, I am certain. I have no idea when Jesus Christ will return and I can't tell you when and how the Rapture of the Church will take place. Anyone who offers up such details about what cannot be known is mistaken - or worse. The Word is clear; **no one knows the day or the time.** No one.

Jesus said, *"Blessed are those servants whom the master, when he comes, will find watching. Hypocrites! You can discern the face of the sky and of the earth, but how is it you do not discern this time?"* - Luke 12:37, 56

Have you ever wondered if Satan knows the day or time when Jesus Christ will return? The Bible says that no one, not even the Son knows - but only the Father in heaven. That means that the Enemy must wait and watch just as we do. It has been suggested that there has been an antichrist waiting to serve Satan in every generation since the Church began in the first century. Because Satan doesn't know the day or time of Christ's return he has had someone standing by in every era, ready to move onto the world stage to serve his evil purpose when needed.

Signs of the End Time

Natural disasters, armed conflicts, and civil disobedience have become the norm since 2011 rather than the exception. Fire, flood, storm, famine, genocide, nuclear accident, war, and 'Occupy' movements; the 24-hour news cycle can't begin to cover the height and breadth of disaster, destruction, and societal dissolution raging across the planet.

God has used earthquakes as a display of His anger or judgment throughout scriptural history. The purpose of natural disasters in this present time may be aligned with God's revelation to Elijah in 1 Kings 19:11-13:

"Then He said, 'Go out, and stand on the mountain before the LORD.' And behold, the LORD passed by, and a great and strong wind tore into the mountains and broke the rocks in pieces before the LORD, but the LORD was not in the wind; and after the wind an earthquake, but the LORD was not in the earthquake; and after the earthquake a fire, but the LORD was not in the fire; and after the fire a still small voice."

*So it was, when Elijah heard it, that he wrapped his face in his mantle and went out and stood in the entrance of the cave. Suddenly a voice came to him, and said, **"What are you doing here, Elijah?"***

We are witness to earthquakes and fire. Amid the quakes, storms, and conflicts this same question is being asked of each of us, "What are you doing here?" The great evangelist Billy Graham once said, "The greatest strike of our generation has not been by labor unions, but by twentieth century Christians, the Army of God which has refused to follow the Savior's commands."

What are you doing here? Are you being obedient to that heavenly vision or just doing your own thing? Do you hear the Shepherd's voice or are you listening to the praise and worship band record their latest arrangement? Did you hear that the King *is* coming?

Jesus Christ is coming. But first He will call His flock to return to the fold. Will you go or will you refuse to obey the still small voice that promises eternal life? Are you ready? Are you sure?

Natural Disasters and the Normalization of Evil

Sendai, Japan was devastated by an 8.9 magnitude earthquake on Friday, March 11, 2011. That was the day the focus of our ministry narrowed. When God draws a line in the sand it is both permanent and non-negotiable.

[19]

Billy Graham's daughter Anne had a similar experience on the morning of September 11, 2001.

"I have held the conviction ... that if I live out my natural lifetime, I will live to see the physical return of Jesus to earth... The burden is so heavy and the vision is so clear that at times life around me seems surreal. I see people sleepwalking when they should be on high alert - their eyes blinded, ears deafened, minds numbed, and hearts hardened to warnings such as 9/11. Warnings so loud they should wake the spiritually dead. Yet many sleep on in lethargy, complacency, apathy ... and just plain denial." - Anne Graham Lotz, *Expecting to See Jesus*, pp.16-17

End Time Prophecy

What is the meaning of the earthquake, fires, floods, and other natural disasters being visited upon the earth? God is not in the disasters. The still small voice calling to the people is His. If we cannot close our ears and eyes to the noise and distraction of these temporal events we will be unable to concentrate and hear what He is saying.

The Shepherd is calling his flock to return to the fold. Do you hear His voice?

"Watch God's cyclones. The only way God sows His saints is by His whirlwind." ~ Oswald Chambers

Today the wind of the Spirit is blowing at gale force. Are you paying attention or have you pulled the covers up over your head, singing "Jesus loves me" in some mad mixture of hope and fear?

Events Signaling the End Times

- Tunisia's Peoples Revolution kicked off 2011
- Mississippi – 7 confirmed tornadoes January 1, 2011
- Australian cyclone and wildfires – January 2011
- Pakistan 7.2 earthquake – January 19, 2011
- Egypt uprising – January 25, 2011
- Yemen revolt – January 27, 2011
- Democrat Senators flee Wisconsin Union Divide – February 16, 2011
- Union protests spread to Ohio, Idaho, Tennessee, etc. – February/March 2011
- Christchurch New Zealand earthquake – February 22, 2011
- Libya opposes Qaddafi – February 26, 2011
- Deadly Texas wildfire scorches more than 110,000 acres – February 27, 2011
- Louisiana tornado brings death – March 5, 2011
- New England record snowfall and flooding – March 7, 2011
- Yunnan, China 5.4 earthquake – March 10, 2011
- Sendai Japanese 8.9 earthquake – March 11, 2011
- Eastern seaboard flooding from Maine to Maryland – March 11, 2011
- Tornadoes that devastated Alabama and the south - a record number
- Mississippi River flooding of May 2011, the most severe since 1937

This short list includes disasters that are all from a six month period of time. Since then we have experienced complete regime changes in the countries surrounding Israel, the impending collapse of European economies, and our own social, political, natural, and financial wake-up call in the United States.

"Do you have the time?"

The End Time is here. If you have been balancing on the thin fence rail between Genesis 1 and Revelation 22, wondering where the world is in the timeline of mankind, I am bluntly stating that the fence is about to break and you must choose which side to fall on. You must choose now.

What does God need to do to get your attention? Does an earthquake have to split your home down the middle? Would a centuries old tree sticking through your roof like a dart in the bulls-eye of a target wake you up? Will you have to fight for breath above the flood water in your own living room before you recognize the time?

If Jesus Christ raptures the church tomorrow are you absolutely sure you will meet Him or do you only hope you will be among that body? If you have even one iota of fear or if you have any doubt at all that you will be included in the Rapture - then I pray *Rapture and Revelation* will be a wise investment of your time.

Nothing in this message is denominational or separated from scripture. Only the Holy Spirit reveals and interprets truth for Christians.

"But the natural man does not receive the things of the Spirit of God, for they are foolishness to him; nor can he know them, because they are spiritually discerned." - 1 Corinthians 2:14

And you ask, "What does all this have to do with me?"

If this should be the day and this the hour that Christ calls His church to meet Him in the air, will you be raptured or will you remain tethered to earth by your wrong choices?

'God' or 'Not God'

The only thing that separates any man or woman from perfect relationship with Christ is a simple choice between two options. When you sift down to the very bottom of any discussion, argument, conversation, or battle, all that remains is one simple choice.

You must choose, **God** or **Not God**.

What part of that simple choice could be misunderstood? You choose God or you don't. No one else's opinion matters -- it's just you and the One Who created the universe. Every decision, belief, relationship, and every crossroad in life eventually distills down to the essential question, "Do you choose God or Not God?"

Many Christians might blurt out without even thinking, "Of course I choose God!" If that were true there would be no fear, no depression, and no doubt. There would be no division in church or family. Yet, all these things exist and seem to be more the norm than the exception.

Most actions, words, and events you will witness are examples of choosing Not God. Many, or most, of the choices made by self-identified Christians are more of the same. Is the god you choose a real being or an impersonal concept of deity? How can you be sure?

Many things Christians assume to be part of scripture are nowhere to be found in the pages between Genesis and Revelation. A thought or concept repeated often enough takes on the attribute of truth even when there is no word from God to support it.

[23]

Where in the Bible can you find the word Rapture? You can't. Where in the Bible do you find the word Trinity? You won't. The word Rapture may not be found in the Bible but there is ample evidence that Jesus will call us from the world before the Tribulation. The Apostles believed it and so do I. The word Trinity may not be in the Bible but there are many references to the Father, Son, and Spirit. Both of these descriptive terms have earned a place in our conversation about, and relationship with, God.

Unless you know why you believe what you believe, the hope of Rapture is simply that. Is your hope founded on faith in what is absolutely true or on what may be nothing more than fable or propaganda? Most false teachers don't realize that the words they profess with complete conviction are not words from God.

Motive aside, the end result of false teaching will be the same. False doctrine = No ticket to Rapture. God has made Himself known. His Spirit lives within each of us. No one is responsible for my salvation except me and no one is responsible for your salvation except you.

Christ simply asks us to "Come as little children." In order to do so we must return to the only credible source for truth - the Word of God.

"Blessed is he who reads and those who hear the words of this prophecy, and keep those things which are written in it; for the time is near. Behold, He is coming with clouds, and every eye will see Him." - Revelation 1:3, 7

The world is on fire.

Thus says the Lord GOD: "Behold, I will kindle a fire in you, and it shall devour every green tree and every dry tree in you; the blazing flame shall not be quenched, and all faces from the south to the

[24]

*north shall be scorched by it. All flesh shall see that I, the LORD,
have kindled it; it shall not be quenched."* - Ezekiel 20:47-48

The world *is* on fire. Not only is the world on fire but there is no
fence upon which you may safely perch until time and circumstance
forces you to one side or the other. Choosing God is choosing life.
The choice of Not God lands you right in the middle of the hottest
flame.

*"But of that day and hour no one knows, not even the angels of
heaven, but My Father only. But as the days of Noah were, so also
will the coming of the Son of Man be. For as in the days before the
flood, they were eating and drinking, marrying and giving in
marriage, until the day that Noah entered the ark, and did not know
until the flood came and took them all away, so also will the coming
of the Son of Man be. Then two men will be in the field: one will be
taken and the other left. Two women will be grinding at the mill: one
will be taken and the other left. Watch therefore, for you do not know
what hour your Lord is coming."* - Matthew 24:37-42

Noah's neighbors went blissfully about their normal lives as he
sweated over each beam and measured each cubit. Imagine what the
locals thought when Noah warned them of the impending flood.

"Noah, you fool."

*"Water from the sky? What have you been chewing on, you
madman?"*

*"Friend, do you see what our neighbor, Noah, is up to? He is
building a monument to his delusion."*

And the rain began to fall and the ark began to float.

I bet there were some nice folks who knew Noah and his family. Maybe there were a few who almost believed his fantastic stories of water falling from the heavens and wondered if they should take him seriously. How many fence-sitters do you suppose Noah knew?

How many fence-sitters do *you* know? The more important question is, "Are you perched on the top rail waiting for a sign to move you to one side or the other?" Well, in the words of Blue Collar comedian Bill Engval, "Here's your sign." Even if the entire population of Noah's world thought the old ark builder just might be right it is obvious that none of them left that seat on the fence until the water carried them away.

The world is like a burning barn. Fine wisps of smoke are beginning to create contrails of sediment in the sunrays that fall across the earth's surface, dancing like dust motes in the light of a west window at eventide. Do you see them yet?

Noah's neighbors perished when the water level rose across the surface of the earth. First the foothills disappeared beneath the waves, then finally the tallest mountain peak. Just as surely as those who ridiculed Noah drowned, people caught in the flames of this world will die as well.

The Burning Barn

The world is a mess. Jesus spoke of His death and said the disciples would *weep and lament*, but that soon their sorrow would turn to joy.

Each day moves us closer to the day Christ calls us home. Each day the world becomes less tolerant of God's people. Each day our numbers seem to be fewer. Yet each day we rejoice in the knowledge that something more wonderful than mortal minds can imagine awaits beyond this day.

[26]

News stories about burning barns usually report the sad fact that horses died in the blaze. Even when a rescuer bravely runs into the barn to save them, many horses are burned alive because they prefer to stay in the safety of their stalls rather than follow someone they don't trust from flame to freedom.

The world is burning. How safe is your place in the world? I assure you, the fire will continue to advance as it greedily inhales the oxygen of sin in this generation. If you take comfort in religion -- don't. Religion is how men share their faith with one another, not how any one man shares his faith with God.

"But the day of the Lord will come as a thief in the night, in which the heavens will pass away with a great noise, and the elements will melt with fervent heat; both the earth and the works that are in it will be burned up." - 2 Peter 3:10

Relationship Saves, Religion Destroys

Religion does not save. Right relationship with Jesus Christ will.

Once a barn is actively involved and flames dance from gatepost to gable there is only one thing that is capable of saving horses trapped in their stalls - relationship with a worthy leader. Horses trapped in a burning barn will remain in their stalls to die unless their faith in the one who comes to lead them out is greater than their fear of the fire. Bo is one of my amazing grays. He is a gray quarter horse gelding I bought as a project when he was two and a half years old and not even halter broke. There would be no Amazing Grays Ministry if not for Bo and my other amazing gray, Swizzle.

I told Bo on the first day of our relationship that I am a worthy leader, that I am always in control and that I will never lie to him. Every day since I have to be sure I live up to those promises. There

[27]

is nothing on earth Bo has to fear as long as I am there to order his world. Part of my leadership includes building his confidence, respecting his equine nature, and helping him become bold, balanced, and fearless.

The test of our relationship is whether Bo's faith in me would be sufficient to overcome his natural fear of fire. If our barn were to burn would Bo leave his stall and follow me out because he trusts me more than he fears the flames? When Bo and I are in right relationship I have no doubt that he would. Our relationship is strong and built on truth and unshakable commitment. The only thing what could save Bo's life in a barn fire is the quality of our relationship.

Relationship with Jesus saves, religion does not. Religion would be me sending you into the burning barn to bring Bo out by simply using my name. "Just tell Bo I said he should go with you." Bo wouldn't buy that line. Bo would perish.

Bo's faith is in me, not an agent who speaks in my name. Have you put your faith in anyone or anything other than Jesus Christ? The only thing that will save you from this burning world is the quality of your personal relationship with Him.

Do you hear the Shepherd's voice or are you simply hoping that you will when the moment of crisis comes? The moment of crisis is here. Is your faith in Jesus Christ so real to you that you will step out on faith even when your eyes, ears, and those around you are telling you to stay in the burning barn?

Zero-Based Christianity

"For the time will come when they will not endure sound doctrine, but according to their own desires, because they have itching ears, they will heap up for themselves teachers; and they will turn their ears away from the truth, and be turned aside to fables."
- 2 Timothy 4:3-4

Why you believe *what* you believe is a matter of life and death. From the moment you spoke your first word the memory banks in your brain have accumulated truth, tradition, assumptions, fables, bad translations, and false teaching.

Much, or most, of what you think you know to be true may be inaccurate or just plain false. When it comes to faith there is only one reliable source, the Word of God interpreted to each child of the King by the Holy Spirit. That's it. There is no second way. Who isn't looking for more faith as the reality of the End Time begins to sink in? The best way to increase the level of your faith in *what* you believe is to know *why* you believe it.

The ultimate authority is the Bible, the inerrant and inspired word of God.

The Devil is in the Details

Zero-Based Christianity is the term I use to describe the process of judging every notion, assumption, and "truth" against the Word of God. If you're familiar with zero-based budgeting you already know what I mean.

The core concepts of faith may be simple, but communicating them well can be a bit more challenging. Especially when you realize that familiar words and what they mean have been hijacked by recent cultural shifts. Sometimes the profound lies within the particular. In other words, bridging the distance between heaven and earth may depend upon the difference between what a word used to mean and its definition today.

Words you have been familiar with since you began recording memories may not mean the same thing to you as they do to your neighbor. These words are so recognizable that you didn't notice when the definition and connotation of those words changed from being cozy, descriptive, humble, and welcome language servants to being useless and divisive baggage.

Five Troublesome 21st Century Words

The essence of these five words began to shift in the 20th century. You may think you know what such familiar words mean, but do you really?

- God
- Jesus
- Christian
- Grace
- Antichrist

The form of the word 'God' that begins with a capital letter has only one meaning. That's my opinion. Not everyone shares that opinion. But you will either absolutely agree that there is only one identity for 'God' or you will not.

Each of these five words used to mean the same thing to most folks which made communication reasonably simple. Unfortunately, none of these five words has a common definition today which makes speaking or debating issues of politics, culture, or faith a real mess.

The Case for Absolute Truth

Before moving on we need to talk about the concept of *absolutes*. Believing in absolutes requires you to accept that if anything is absolutely true then the opposite must be absolutely false. Likewise, if anything is absolutely right then the opposite must be absolutely wrong.

Dr. Francis Schaeffer (1912-1984), an influential theologian, author, and pastor, took on the concept of absolute truth in his 1968 book, *The God Who is There*. I found the depth of Dr. Schaeffer's work a little overwhelming at times as he explained in great detail and with a wealth of citations, how and when men and women began to develop their post-Christian intellectual positions.

Dr. Schaeffer's works are mines with deep veins of intellectual ore. It was not unusual for me to read, re-read, and re-re-read parts of his books just trying to get a firm grip on the foundation and truth of the formulas he uses to communicate social and personal change relative to the constancy of God.

The chaotic state of our homes, churches, communities, nations, and world are more easily understood when you discover what different people think about this question of absolutes. I don't know exactly how many people in the United States believe in absolutes and how many do not. I expect most people wouldn't know the answer to the question if I asked them.

Truth is truth. You will only agree with this statement if you accept the existence of absolutes. If something is true then it is always true and must therefore be true in every situation. C.S. Lewis also wrote about truth and how mankind has progressively relegated belief in the possibility of absolute truths to the rubbish bin.

"Your man has been accustomed, ever since he was a boy, to have a dozen incompatible philosophies dancing about together inside his head. He doesn't think of doctrines as primarily 'true' or 'false', but as 'academic' or 'practical', 'outworn' or 'contemporary', 'conventional' or 'ruthless'. Jargon, not argument, is your best ally in keeping him from the Church." -- C.S. Lewis, *The Screwtape Letters*

As you consider this short list of absolutes you will begin to see the magnitude of the problem for Christians trying to live in the secular world, or even a "religious" world that refuses to admit that absolutes exist.

Absolute Concepts

- God (Jehovah) absolutely exists or He does not.

- Gay marriage is absolutely wrong or it is not.

- Pedophilia is absolutely wrong or it is not.

- Stealing is absolutely wrong or it is not.

- Children are born of a man and a woman or they are not.

- Every race is absolutely equal to every other race or it is not.

- Cheating is absolutely wrong or it is not.

- Abortion is absolutely wrong or it is not.

- Life absolutely begins at conception or it does not.

- Jesus is both fully human and fully divine or He is not.

- Jesus Christ is the only way to heaven or He is not.

- The Bible is either absolutely true or it is not

What did you think as you read down this list of absolutes? Do you agree that absolutes exist or would you suggest another option or exception to these antiquated ideas of right and wrong?

Major Christian denominations argue the deity of Jesus Christ. Others consider matters of abortion or homosexuality to be relative and not absolutely right or wrong.

The general morality of the United States today provides a perfect example of a society that has rejected absolutes. Very little (if anything) is considered absolutely true or absolutely false. Recognizing this fact leads us back to the very first item on our list of absolutes -- does God exist or does He not?

It is easy to discuss most issues if you have agreement in the existence of absolutes. Unfortunately, general agreement about absolutes no longer exists because there is no longer agreement on the existence of God.

The simplest way to make a distinction between what these five words used to mean and how they are used today is to separate concepts by using the capitalized form of each word differently than the form of the word expressed in all lower case letters.

I'll explain what I mean using the word 'jenny.' Jenny is the name of a friend's six-year old daughter. A jenny is also the general term that identifies a female donkey. The capitalized form of the word refers to a specific person while the lower case form means something general, non-unique, and non-specific.

[33]

Here's another example that may help you follow what's coming next. What about the word bible? Are you sure you know what it means when you hear it used in a conversation?

Bible definitions:

Bible - to a Protestant the Bible is the Old and New Testaments.

Bible - to a Catholic the Bible is the New Testament and the Old Testament with the additional books of *1st* and *2nd Maccabees*, *Baruch, Tobit, Judith, The Wisdom of Solomon, Sirach*, additions to *Esther*, and the stories of *Susanna* and *Bel and the Dragon* which are included in *Daniel*. Orthodox Old Testaments include these plus *1st* and *2nd Esdras, Prayer of Manasseh, Psalm 151* and *3rd Maccabees*.

Bible - to a Jew the Bible is the Hebrew version of the Old Testament which is different from either of the Protestant and Catholic versions

So you see, the word Bible, even when used to describe the written Word of God is not defined in the same way by everyone.

Understanding the difference between God and god

How prevalent is the belief that God is who or what you think He is? How many times have you heard this very politically correct statement; "You have your god and I have mine. As long as you are happy with yours, who am I to say you're wrong; just leave me and my god alone."

"I believe in God." is a far different statement than "I believe in god (or a god.)"

The first three of the Ten Commandments address the identity and unique deity of God. The Old Testament has at least seventeen unique names for God including Elohim, Adonai, and Jehovah - Yahweh. God is the author of creation and the Word. There is one God. That one God is called Father by Jesus Christ, a real man in actual world history who is both wholly divine and wholly human.

It has become fashionable for different denominations to make their god of the Bible genderless. Their god is no longer God the Father, but god the father/mother/neuter. Jesus Christ identifies His Father many times in the New Testament. If the heart of Christianity is Jesus Christ, wouldn't you think that folks who consider themselves Christians would accept Jesus' testimony that God is indeed His Father?

"I am the LORD, and there is no other;
There is no God besides Me."

"Assemble yourselves and come;
Draw near together,
You who have escaped from the nations.
They have no knowledge,
Who carry the wood of their carved image,
And pray to a god that cannot save.
Tell and bring forth your case;
Yes, let them take counsel together.
Who has declared this from ancient time?
Who has told it from that time?
Have not I, the LORD?
And there is no other God besides Me,
A just God and a Savior;
There is none besides Me. - Isaiah 45: 5, 20-21

[35]

Isaiah chapter 45 repeats at least nine times, "I am God. There is no other." Allah is not God. There is no God but Jehovah, the God who created all that is.

Dr. Schaeffer's title says it all, *The God Who Is There*. The God of the Bible, the Father who sent Jesus to redeem us, is God who is actually real. He is there. He is everywhere. He is.

"Whenever men say they are looking for greater reality, we must show them at once the reality of true Christianity. This is real because it is concerned with the God who is there and who has spoken to us about Himself, not just the use of the symbol god or christ which sounds spiritual but is not."- Dr. Frances Schaeffer, *The God Who is There*, pg. 61

The God of true Christianity has identified Himself, quantified the relationship we have with Him, provided the means for our salvation, and promised eternal reunion in a new heaven and new earth. Any god other than this God is just a symbol. The only way to find out what someone means when they say "god" today is to ask.

It's tricky business when a "Christian" refers to god who is either less or more than what the Bible says God is. If someone believes any part of the Bible to be untrue then their god is not the God who gave Moses the Law or gave His Son to die for our sins.

There is absolutely one God. He told us He is the only god. If the God of the Bible absolutely exists then there can absolutely be no other god.

Just as there will be many false christ's [Mark 13:22] there are many false gods worshipped by "Christians." Is there a god who approves gay marriage? I know there is because I've been told it by the folks who believe in him/her/it. But their god did not speak the universe into creation. Their god is not really present.

Zero-based Christianity begins and ends with the God who is there and who speaks to us through His Word and Spirit. There is only one God or there is not. If there is not, then no god exists with any power other than that conferred upon him/her/it by humans.

Who is your god? Whoever preaches or teaches any god other than the God of the Bible is a false teacher by intention or error.

Understanding the difference between Jesus and jesus

The Bible has but one subject -- Jesus Christ. From creation to Abraham, Egypt to Bethlehem, and Calvary to the New Jerusalem, everything was, is, and will be about Jesus.

The Bible also has many names for Jesus. He is God, Lord, Messiah, Alpha and Omega, Bright Morning Star, Redeemer, Lamb of God, Light of the World, and Savior. Any reference to a jesus who is not this Jesus is not Jesus.

I read the best-selling novels *The Shack* and *The DaVinci Code* for the same reason; so I would be able to separate what was hype from the truth.

The jesus of *The DaVinci Code*

A few years ago this blockbuster novel by Dan Brown swept theatres, communities, and churches across the globe. I have never seen a better example of blasphemy than *The DaVinvi Code*. Doubts created by reading this book disturbed the peace of many Christians whose feet weren't set into a spiritual rock of faith.

Readers and movie-goers started to question whether Jesus was who and what they had always been led to believe He was. Was Jesus really divine? Did Jesus marry Mary Magdalene and father a daughter, the Holy Grail? What part did the Catholic Church play in any cover-up of the real history and death of Jesus of Nazareth? Is the Bible a lie?

The DaVinci Code is a masterful tapestry of facts and lies woven together so skillfully that the finished picture fooled many into thinking it was all true. One of the first pages in the book even states that the contents are true. The jesus of *The DaVinci Code* is not Jesus of Nazareth, Prince of Peace, Son of the Living God, and the One who will judge each of us in a day not too far off. This jesus is not divine. This jesus is a lie.

"Beloved, do not believe every spirit, but test the spirits, whether they are of God; because many false prophets have gone out into the world." - 1 John 4:1

The Bible clearly tells us that many false jesus' will be used to promote the lies of Satan. How do you know that all you've read and heard about Jesus over the years is true?

The "Jesus" of *The Shack*

Is *The Shack* a beautiful story that offers readers the vision of a more profound relationship with Jesus Christ, God the Father, and the Holy Spirit? Or is *The Shack* a lie dressed up in very pretty clothes and sprinkled with fairy dust and sweet perfume?

The Shack offers a few really wonderful glimpses into the true Grace and love of God. However, the book gives a completely false picture of salvation. It implies that everyone will go to heaven because "God" loves all of his/her children too much to condemn them. The jesus who is given words by the author tells the main character that there are many paths to heaven.

One of the most powerful messages in *The Shack* is also powerfully wrong. "God" appears as a middle-aged woman dressed in judicial robes who tells the main character, Mack, *"You must choose two of your [five] children to spend eternity in God's new heavens and new earth, but only two. And you must choose three of your children to spend eternity in hell."*

Mack couldn't believe what he was hearing and began to panic until the god figure explained, *"I am only asking you to do something that you believe God does."*

The character is aghast that he might have to sentence some of his children to hell. The author finished this section by saying that God sees it the same way and would never do such a thing. *"And now you know Papa's heart, who loves all his children perfectly."*

What a silly comparison. The message would be more scriptural if it showed all five of Mack's children hanging out a second story window as the building is consumed with flames. Imagine Mack calling to his children to trust him and jump into his arms. Those with faith in their father would jump and be spared. Those with no faith and chose to stay in the building will burn.

The Shack would have you believe that most Christians think that God picks which ones to catch and which ones to leave in the burning building regardless of their actions or lack of action. God the Father doesn't do that. Like the father in my illustration, all our Father can do when his children are in danger is to offer rescue based upon their faith in him. Each child must decide for himself.

No matter the crime, no matter the refusal, *The Shack* implies that every person will be forgiven even if he or she doesn't particularly want forgiveness. This message is not Biblical.

Jesus of Nazareth is absolutely God or he is not. Jesus is a real flesh-and-blood human who was born into the world from outside the world. Jesus was born, died, was resurrected, ascended, and lives forever in glory. Jesus is God.

There is only one Jesus who can save you. This is Jesus who is with us and has spoken to us about Himself. This Jesus is one with God the Father. When you hear that "Jesus never said anything about it" as an excuse for sin, ask yourself whether God ever said anything about the matter. Jesus and God are one and the same. Whatever God said Jesus said.

Who is this jesus that we hear so much about today who loves all, judges none, believes in taxing the wealthy, and is a political liberal? This jesus is a concept fabricated by Humanists at best and a demon in shepherd's robes at worst.

This convenient jesus is led about like a lapdog, dressed in whatever costume the situation calls for to persuade or mislead the uninformed and the gullible. It is this jesus that artists malign and social progressives quote.

The President of the United States told an audience in February 2012 that jesus would raise taxes if he were here. The jesus he referred to has no power to raise taxes much less save sinners. The Jesus who is here is not concerned with the minutiae of the world, but rather the details that makes up the lives of his children.

Jesus is here inasmuch as He lives within you and me. Jesus the Savior is no longer of this world and has no interest in politics or taxes. Jesus will be returning and you need to know Jesus of Nazareth, not one of the jesus-symbols being used to bolster the false doctrines that make up the majority of Christian-speak today.

What did Jesus Say?

The fad of W.W.J.D. bracelets and its rhetoric is used to deceive more than to save. The question for Christians has never been "What would Jesus do." The pertinent question has always been, "What did Jesus say?"

The record of what Jesus said is clear. Have you ever read the Bible and tried to answer the questions Jesus asked? Here are twelve questions Jesus asked as He walked with real men on real dirt roads in real time and under a real sun.

1. Can any of you by worrying add a single moment to your lifespan? (Matthew 6:27)
2. To what shall I compare this generation? (Matthew 11:6)
3. Did you never read the scriptures? (Matthew 21:42)
4. Why this commotion and weeping? (Mark 5:39)
5. Why do you call me 'Lord, Lord' and not do what I command? (Luke 6:46)
6. Where is your faith? (Luke 8:25)
7. If even the smallest things are beyond your control, why are you anxious about the rest? (Luke 12:26)
8. But when the Son of Man comes, will He find any faith on earth? (Luke 18:8)
9. If I tell you about earthly things and you will not believe, how will you believe when I tell you of heavenly things? (John 3: 12)
10. Do you realize what I have done for you? (John 13:12)
11. Have I been with you for so long and still you do not know Me? (John 14:9)
12. Do you love Me? (John 21:16)

There is only one Jesus. Any preaching or teaching about a jesus that contradicts the Bible is not Jesus, but a puppet-jesus who is not real and has no power to save.

Jesus posed this question in Matthew 16:15,"Who do you say I am?" *Who* do you believe Jesus is and *why* do you believe what you believe?

Understanding the difference between Christian and christian

The next word to consider is "Christian." C.S. Lewis wrote the forward to *Mere Christianity* around 1952. In the Preface Lewis wrote, *"*Now if once we allow people to start spiritualizing and refining, or as they might say 'deepening' the sense of the word Christian, it will speedily become a useless word."

Rather than erring on the side of stricter definition, history proves that we took the other fork in the road and broadened the accepted meaning of the word Christian to include good folks, moral folks, and people who think Jesus was simply a pretty good guy.

The result is exactly what Lewis predicted, though for an entirely different reason. Various sources quantify the variations among Christians. Not only are there the obvious distinctions like Catholics and Protestants, but there are subgroups within each major denomination and new churches continue to spring up because the founding members interpret Christianity just a little differently than everyone else. It simply isn't possible to have hundreds of different types of Christians. It is, however, entirely possible to have 800 different types of christians.

Lewis was making the point that the only true distinction that may be rightfully made is between one who is a Christian and one who is not. Being a Christian is an absolute; there are no degrees. Relationship with Jesus Christ cannot be ordered like a sandwich from Burger King where you can "have it your way."

Kleenex®, Band-Aids®, and Coke® are specific products even though the words themselves have become generic over the years. Any facial tissue may be called kleenex. A small adhesive bandage is generically called a band aid. And in parts of the country every soft drink is called a coke.

In many circles it is unchristian to suggest that really nice people who are generous with others and who serve as great role models for children and adults alike will not be allowed entrance into heaven just because they do not confess Jesus Christ as Lord and Savior. The problem we face today is that the word 'christian' is accepted as an accurate label for moral people with good behavior but who do not have a personal relationship with Christ.

Christians

There are many more christians in the world today than Christians. Christians believe the Bible is the infallible and inerrant word of God and that Jesus of Nazareth is the Word made flesh.

In very simple terms a Christian confesses God and Jesus, not a god and a jesus.

"For he was a good man, full of the Holy Spirit and of faith. And a great many people were added to the Lord. Then Barnabas departed for Tarsus to seek Saul. And when he had found him, he brought him to Antioch. So it was that for a whole year they assembled with the church and taught a great many people. And the disciples were first called Christians in Antioch." - Acts 11:24-26

[43]

The first time the label "Christian" was used was shortly after Jesus ascended to sit at His Father's right hand. Christians have but one master, our Lord and Savior, Jesus Christ.

Christians believe that all history revolves around one single event - the death of an historical Jesus Christ on a real cross on a real hillside. Christians believe Jesus literally arose on the third day. Christians believe Jesus died that their sins could be forgiven and allow entrance into the presence of Almighty God. Christians believe Jesus came into the world from outside of the world as both fully human and fully divine.

Christians are by definition new creations - visibly and demonstrably different from their former selves and from the world around them. Christians live in the world but are not of the world, knowing that their citizenship is in heaven and not on earth. [Philippians 3:20]

The symbolic christian seeks goodwill and fellowship with all. They judge both themselves and others by general rules of conduct and morality. They are "nice" people for the most part. Some are truly exceptional people, deserving of the respect and admiration of their neighbors.

The symbolic christian often goes along to get along. Compromise is always an option for christians when opposing viewpoints face off across the table. The ends justify the means for christians. They believe good goals can be accomplished even when the tactics needed to get there are a bit sketchy.

The symbolic christian celebrates tolerance and the concept of individual truth. "What's true for you may be different from what is true for me."

Christians accept only one truth which, by definition, must be true in every situation and circumstance. Recent Barna Group studies discovered that only 7% of Americans believe that the Bible is the true and inerrant Word of God. Another Barna report dated May 2009 found that 80% of born again Christians agree that spiritual maturity may be defined as "trying hard to follow the rules."

When did the gospel message of salvation become "just try hard to follow the rules"? These christians have been reborn into a relationship with jesus, not Jesus. Since jesus is a product of their imagination such "rebirth" is meaningless.

Who preached the lie that salvation is granted by "trying hard"? False prophets today teach their congregations about a jesus who died for nothing. This jesus did not die. This jesus does not save. This jesus is absolutely a lie.

"Enter by the narrow gate; for wide is the gate and broad is the way that leads to destruction, and there are many who go in by it. Because narrow is the gate and difficult is the way which leads to life, and there are few who find it. Beware of false prophets, who come to you in sheep's clothing, but inwardly they are ravenous wolves." - Matthew 7:13-15

Christians celebrate relationship with Christ. Christians do not debate what is not debatable; they do not compromise and allow evil to sit at the same table as good. A *christian* does good works because it's the **moral thing** to do. Christians do the will of God because it's the **only thing** to do.

In this End Time Christians are being ejected from churches and assemblies populated by christians who mistakenly think they're being righteous by clearing out the bad seeds. Many churches today are far more comfortable welcoming brothers and sisters in sin rather than brothers and sisters in Christ. It is far easier to welcome someone who is actively sinning rather than a precious saint who sacrifices self to Christ. It is far easier to feel superior to a sinner than a saint. But then again, feeling superior to anyone is not a Christian characteristic.

"They will put you out of the synagogues, yes, the time is coming that whoever kills you will think that he offers God service. And these things they will do to you because they have not known the Father nor Me." - John 16:2-3

Christianity is about relationship with a real Jesus. You are either one with the body of Jesus Christ or you are not. There is no middle ground and no rail to balance on while you consider your options. There is no more time on the clock. The divide grows between those of this world and those who look forward to the next. Sitting on the fence is an absolute choice to *not* follow Christ.

Understanding the difference between Grace and grace

Biblical Grace is the free gift of redemption based upon the unmerited and undeserved favor bestowed upon a sinner by a loving God. Jesus paid a debt he did not owe to cover a debt we could not pay. That is Grace.

Grace scriptures:

- *For the law was given through Moses, but grace and truth came through Jesus Christ.* - John 1:17

- *Now to him who works, the wages are not counted as grace but as debt.* - Romans 4:4

- *And He said to me, "My grace is sufficient for you, for My strength is made perfect in weakness."* - 2 Corinthians 12:9

[46]

- *I do not set aside the grace of God; for if righteousness comes through the law, then Christ died in vain."* - Galatians 2:21

- *For by grace you have been saved through faith, and that not of yourselves; it is the gift of God,* - Ephesians 2:8

Eric Metaxas' biography of Dietrich Bonhoeffer (1906-1945) sums up his life and death in the book's subtitle, "Pastor, Martyr, Prophet, Spy." Bonhoeffer dedicated his life to the pursuit of Christ and was martyred at the hand of Adolf Hitler for being faithful to the truth of the gospel.

"Cheap grace is preaching forgiveness without requiring repentance, baptism without church discipline, Communion without confession. ... Cheap grace is grace without discipleship, grace without the cross, grace without Jesus Christ, living and incarnate." - Dietrich Bonhoeffer, *The Cost of Discipleship*

Bonhoeffer continues with his description of real grace, "Costly grace confronts us as a gracious call to follow Jesus, it comes as a word of forgiveness to the broken spirit and contrite heart. It is costly because it compels a man to submit to the yoke of Christ and follow him; it is grace because Jesus says: "My yoke is easy and My burden is light."

The doctor who witnessed Bonhoeffer's execution in a German concentration camp wrote: "I saw Pastor Bonhoeffer ... kneeling on the floor praying fervently to God. I was most deeply moved by the way this lovable man prayed, so devout and so certain that God heard his prayer. At the place of execution, he again said a short prayer and then climbed the few steps to the gallows, brave and composed. His death ensued after a few seconds. In the almost fifty

[47]

years that I worked as a doctor, I have hardly ever seen a man die so entirely submissive to the will of God."

The grace being preached in many churches today sounds something like this, "Of course you have sinned, but now everything is forgiven. You don't have to change, just stay as you are and enjoy the consolation of free forgiveness."

Dietrich Bonhoeffer understood Grace. The Grace given freely by Jesus Christ is neither cheap nor free; this Grace cost the Father his only Son.

How many "Christians" have been taught that grace is distributed freely to every comer whether holy or evil? Remember this statement from our discussion about the jesus of *The Shack*? "No matter the crime, no matter the refusal, *The Shack* implies that every person will be forgiven even if he or she doesn't particularly want forgiveness."

Can you think of any better example of cheap grace? The jesus who offers such grace was not born of a virgin, did not minister to the twelve disciples, and is not sitting at the right hand of God the Father.

Costly Grace is given freely to every child of the King of Kings. The only requirement for such costly Grace is relationship with the real God who exists; the real Son who saves; and the real Spirit who lives within you.

Are you wagering your eternity on the cheap grace of god and jesus, or the costly Grace delivered by the blood of Jesus Christ?

[48]

Understanding the Difference between Antichrist and antichrist

Scripture clearly states that the Antichrist will appear in the final days as the flames of a world on fire spread from east to west and north to south. John warns us [1 John 2:18] that it is already the last hour. He laid out before us the error of our sin, lust, and pride that causes us to choose darkness over light.

Who is *the* Antichrist? Judas Iscariot was a type of antichrist. Anyone who leaves his walk by choosing the road with brighter, more intense earthly light given as bait by the Enemy, is an antichrist.

Antichrist is already here

Jesus told us that no one knows the day or hour of his return except the Father. That means Satan doesn't know the time either. The Antichrist-elect is already here. In every generation there had to be one person waiting in the wings prepared for the cue to move onto the world stage. Rest assured, there is someone out there today who may be tapped for the role.

The Antichrist has long been heralded as a player whose arrival announces the last hour. And, John says, many antichrists have already come [1 John 2:28-29] proving that the clock has indeed wound down to our final moments. We have received the truth of Christ and anyone who denies the Father and the Son is, according to scripture, an antichrist. [1John 2:22]

Jesus: Christ and antichrist?

Could Jesus of Nazareth be not only the Christ, but possibly an antichrist as well? Don't leap to any conclusions yet. Stay with me a moment longer and be prepared to compare this theory against both the Bible and your own experience of truth as revealed by the Holy Spirit. No lesson or fact should be accepted as true unless it passes this test.

Please understand, I am not saying Jesus is *the* Antichrist. But in these last days the narrow path to the Kingdom of God is viewed by many in our culture as intolerant, hateful, mean-spirited, tyrannical, unjust, and unloving. To the people who have eyes that do not see and ears that do not hear, the true gospel message is hateful and even evil.

Anti-Christ is Christ-opposite

By definition the Antichrist is Christ-opposite. Jesus Christ who lived, taught for three years, died, and was resurrected is the opposite of the false god and jesus preached by many "persons of faith" today. One of the best examples of this crazy upside-down turn of events is masterfully presented by C.S. Lewis in *The Screwtape Letters*.

Lewis' brilliant exchange of letters between a senior devil and a junior demon offer astonishing insight into the method Satan uses to corrupt humans. The Father (Satan) seeks to keep the soul of each human out of the reach of The Enemy (God.) From the perspective of Satan, Jesus is the true human embodiment of the Antichrist.

Anyone who preaches a false jesus, whether he is aware of it or not, serves the Enemy of Heaven. Any jesus who deviates from the messiahship of Jesus of Nazareth, as both promised and accomplished in scripture, is an antichrist to Jesus in the same way Jesus is an antichrist to those who teach or preach a symbolic jesus who never lived at all.

Christ is the Light of the World; Antichrist is a beacon of darkness. To the worldy who profess god and jesus, Jesus of Nazareth is the antichrist.

I realize this discussion asks you to think outside the box. Understanding the distinctions between God and god; Jesus and jesus; Christian and christian; Grace and grace; may actually help you to better understand your place in the world today and why you feel like an alien in a strange land. "The world does not know us, because it did not know Him." [1 John 3:1]

This false symbol of jesus is used by the Enemy to attack those who confess Jesus Christ, Son of God. This jesus is a type of antichrist because he is the opposite of Christ. The true Christ is the antichrist to those who worship god and jesus and who depend upon a false grace for salvation.

The Antichrist of Revelation is fully human but not divine. He is a pawn being used by his master Satan. The true Christ is fully divine even as He is fully human. The true Christ is no pawn - He is God Himself.

Be vigilant.

Many reveal what they claim they learned while in the spirit. From pulpit to stage to Revival meeting, compare what you hear to God's truth. Not every spirit who speaks to a man is the Holy Spirit. Satan is a liar.

In these End Times it is impossible to communicate the extent of the corruption facing you without making a distinction between God and god; Jesus and jesus; Christians and christians; and Grace and grace. Simply, the capitalized word denotes the Biblical intent of the word and the lower case word is nothing more than how the world has corrupted something worth everything into something worth nothing.

The Name of Jesus is a Stumbling Block of Offense

"Therefore, to you who believe, He is precious; but to those who are disobedient, 'The stone which the builders rejected has become the chief cornerstone,' and 'A stone of stumbling and a rock of offense.'" - 1 Peter 2:7-8

The name of Jesus is sweet and invokes instant security and peace to his flock. We know the voice of our Shepherd and His name is music to our ears.

When you speak the name of Jesus Christ aloud to others you will experience one of two results, (1) connection or (2) rejection. It is acceptable to talk about God and spirituality, but it is not politically correct to include the name of Jesus.

There is no Christianity without Christ. I have no message if there is no Cross of Christ. My books are based on the Bible and there is no other subject of the Bible save Jesus Christ. The name of Jesus is central to the messages of my books. Over the last year or two I have been rejected quite a few times by "Christian" radio programs, etc. for being *too Christian.* In other words, I use the name of Jesus Christ and that name carries a mighty power that either attracts or repels.

It's easy for people to get along when they talk about generic faith in god or in spirituality. Such is the stuff of religion and non-religion. Everyone who speaks of god simply as a Supreme Power is fooling themselves. You cannot have a relationship with a generic god or with an unnamed, unknown Supreme Power.

[53]

Books about faith and spirituality are easier to share when they speak of faith or spirit and refer to some generic "power." But there can be no power if there is no specific Who. To have relationship there must be someone that is the Who and that someone must have a name and identity. The parties to any relationship must be specific individuals for the relationship to have any meaning at all.

Any god who is unknown or unnamed is not the God of the Bible. Jesus Christ is a real person. He was born, grew into manhood, and walked the dusty roads with friends, family, and disciples. Jesus entered the world from outside of the world as deity and as a human. Jesus died a real death on a real calendar day that began when the sun rose in the east and ended when it set in the west. It is possible to have a real relationship with Jesus Christ because He is *real*. There is no substance to relationship with an unnamed supreme being and certainly no power to save.

To have a relationship there must be a *who*. There is no faith that overcomes fear if you can't define the object of your faith. How can someone have faith in something they can't identify? There is only one Name and only one Jesus Christ. Yet the name of Christ is a stumbling block to many. There is power in the name of Jesus Christ and His is the only name with the power to save.

"And you will be hated by all for My name's sake. But he who endures to the end shall be saved." - Mark 13:13

Who are you in relationship with? Ask yourself, *How often do I speak the name of Jesus?* For years I played it safe and spoke only of God. It's still the safe bet to leave Jesus out of your conversation if you seek fellowship with others in the world. But it's a losing bet when the smoke heats up enough for the flames to be seen by all. Jesus will come to lead us from this burning barn of a world.

[54]

For two millennia men have puzzled over the timing of His return because they know that Jesus Christ is the only way out of the flames. All creation is experiencing the rise and fall of prophetic labor pains. Look around you; do you doubt the increasing frequency of the expansion and contraction of nature and human society, of the rhythmic battle being waged as this world moves toward the next?

There is power in only one name - Jesus.

The choice between God and Not God may be reduced to a simpler one, Jesus or Not? Is Jesus the only way or is that doctrine intolerant? Does Jesus support today's liberal policies as some politicians suggest?

The power to save is in the name of Jesus, Son of God. There is nothing but lies in the name of any other jesus.

Living the Gospel in the End Time

Most who profess faith in Jesus Christ have encountered difficulties in relationships with some family members and lifelong friends. If you haven't felt like the odd man out yet, just wait, it's coming. Those who live in the world cannot understand why you aren't the same person you used to be -- back when you were exactly as they still are today.

"What's gotten into you? You're taking this 'Jesus' thing way too seriously. You act like you've been brain-washed. We're really getting worried about you."

New creations in Christ do not participate in lewdness, lusts, drinking parties, and abominable idolatries. [1 Peter 4:3] Dirty dancing is not the Saturday night pursuit of a New Creation. Playing gory video games where the victor splatters his foe all over the place is not a pastime for a child of God.

You won't find a New Creation holding down a bar stool at closing time at the local pub after an evening of window shopping the patrons. As you walk more closely with Jesus you will also find that only a precious few television programs are fit for eyes that look forward to the Rapture.

Friends and family who do not hear the Shepherd's voice will think you're antisocial when you decline to go along with their "flood of dissipation" [1 Peter 4:4] and will speak evil about you if you do not straighten up and fly right again. What are you to do? Peter answers that question by telling us that the end of all things is at hand and we should be serious and watchful in our prayers. [1 Peter 4:7]

[57]

What is true is always true, regardless of the time and the manner in which such truth is conveyed. Careful selection of our friends and associates has always been important. Back in the day this was one of the most important lessons parents tried to teach children. It is a truth that still holds today, but fewer and fewer parents think enough of their children to teach this lesson.

There's a saying I first heard decades ago when I began to study leadership and corporate management. "It's hard to soar with eagles when you fly with a bunch of turkeys."

Remember that one? The sentiment is still true and still relevant, especially for Christians in these times. It has never been as hard to escape the flock of turkeys as it is today. It matters who you spend your time with. It matters what you watch on television. It matters what you read and it matters what you say. There must be a clear contrast between your life and that of friends and family who do not proclaim Jesus as Lord.

Which do you value most, human wisdom or God's wisdom? It is human wisdom, arrogance and idolatry of the self that makes abortion possible. The philosophy (religion) of Humanism elevates the individual to god-like status and admits no greater wisdom than that of men and secular scholarship. In what universe would God consider the murder of an innocent wise? Certainly not the universe described in the first chapter of Genesis.

Are you a citizen of the world or a new creature in Christ Jesus? You have the freedom to chase fame, wealth, women, men, and anything else you find appealing. Choose the world, it's waiting to embrace you. So is Christ, but the choice is either/or. Choose the world and you kiss your eternal future goodbye.

[58]

Worldly people live in uncertainty and fear. History is full of geniuses who committed suicide because they never found the real meaning of life. The world produces despair, disillusionment, and depression. The world has no grace to offer. God does. His Grace produces faith that overcomes fear - right here and right now.

Jesus made one offering to God that forever ended the need for blood sacrifice. By His one offering at Calvary he perfected forever those who are being sanctified. [Hebrews 10:14] The only source of true wisdom is the God of the Bible. Do not be distracted by the shouts and jeers that make up most of public debate and discourse.

Do you seek sin or sanctification? There is no way you can play with Satan's buddies during the day and go home to a house Jesus prepared for you at day's end. [John 14:2] False teachers will preach that you can have both. Some will believe them but don't you fall for that lie.

What should Christians *do* in the End Time?

Not only is this the End Time, but time is quickly running out for those who profess Jesus Christ as Lord to either put up or shut up. I know that's hardly ministry talk, but it makes the point I intend to make. It's decision time. The line in the sand wasn't drawn just for me, but for all Christians. There is no time left on the clock.

Practically speaking, just what should Christians *do* in the end times? Should you quit your job, cash out your 401-K and head to the hills until Jesus calls you to meet him in the air? There are a few basic things that must be attended to in order to be ready:

- Profess Christ as Lord

- Repent of sin and accept the free gift of salvation

- Withdraw from every brother who is disorderly.
  [2 Thessalonians 3:6]

- Be known by your love for others in the family

- Listen to the Master's voice and respond appropriately

There is one thing not to do - sit around like a mushroom day and night, Bible at the ready, waiting for Christ to appear.

"Now when He had spoken these things, while they watched, He was taken up, and a cloud received Him out of their sight. And while they looked steadfastly toward heaven as He went up, behold, two men stood by them in white apparel, who also said, 'Men of Galilee, why do you stand gazing up into heaven? This same Jesus, who was taken up from you into heaven, will so come in like manner as you saw Him go into heaven.'" - Acts 1:9-11

Wouldn't it be silly to stand around waiting for an event that (1) may not happen in your lifetime, or (2) when it does occur you certainly aren't going to miss it? Once you are ready for the Bridegroom all you need do is remain watchful and ready. The most practical thing for a Christian to do in the End Time is to be ready. A profoundly simple truth is that if you are always ready you never have to worry about getting ready.

There are actual discussion groups that debate whether Christians should buy homes or continue educational pursuits in the End Time. Scripture appears to be clear that each of us still has a purpose beyond star-gazing. That purpose certainly isn't to become a lifeless, useless door stop waiting to be picked up by a rapture vacuum.

Every person who loves Jesus Christ is concerned about the direction the world has moved in the past century. If indeed this is the End

Time, do you wonder how your family, your children, or your grandchildren will be affected?

Parental Responsibility for Children and Grandchildren before Rapture

Tiny children believe their parents can do everything and know all there is to know. Tots really think that Dad can bring out the stars at night and Mom knows the words of every song the birds sing. Children with complete faith in their parents have no fear. But the day will come when sons and daughters realize their mothers and fathers are human and imperfect. This is the day they begin to know fear.

Christian parents are responsible to introduce their children to Jesus Christ before they are exposed as flawed humans. When that day arrives and your children learn that you really can't protect them from everything, you must be certain you have faithfully ensured that your sons and daughters know Jesus, the one who is 100% willing and able to care for them.

Just as you have a unique relationship with Jesus Christ so do each of your children and grandchildren. Jesus is perfectly capable of caring for you. He is equally capable of caring for the kids.

In this End Time be sure your family has been introduced to Jesus Christ. Continue to support these vital relationships and the Holy Spirit will do the rest. Remember, you don't know everything and you can't protect anyone else from the future. But Jesus does and Jesus will.

Evil in Everyday Clothing

What can we learn from the civil insurrections of 2011 that originated in Wisconsin over collective-bargaining? Do you remember the thousands of protesters, civil disobedience, destruction of public property, death threats against legislators, and all the elected officials who abandoned their post yet were granted hero status by the mob?

Protesters and innocents alike DIED in Nazi Germany and Middle East uprisings. Did Wisconsin Governor Scott Walker call in the National Guard, or even the Madison police, to spray the protesters with live ammunition or even tear gas? No.

Why is there no such outrage against abortion? Gay marriage? Child pornography? Can it really be true that we'll only turn off the TV and rise from the couch when our pocketbook is threatened?

Open your eyes. The scale of union protests is further evidence that we are in the End Time. "Their eyes will be closed and their ears stopped." The protests that inspire the greatest passion are for gay rights, the environment, and invasion of the wallet. What about freedom to worship? What about abortion? What about protecting our children?

Our government asks for more money, more power, and more labor from the productive citizenry in order to spend more on itself. When most governmental programs are sliced down to their core the worm is revealed. Most of these programs are designed to expand governmental power by further enslaving the population with "entitlements" - a popular word that means "keep me in power." (Entitlements are discussed at length in the chapter titled, Rapture : Theory and Requirements.)

There is lunacy in the present definition of poverty. Jesus Christ said the poor would be with us always. He was not referring to those who had a home, two televisions, a microwave, cable TV and cell phones.

Yet many who are on the government dole today have all these luxuries and more.

What provides discernment for Christians as we evaluate what we hear and see today? Certainly not the particular dogma or creed of any denomination, not the learned rhetoric of any scholar; and not anyone with a microphone or blog who captures your attention; discernment comes through the person of Jesus Christ.

The only way to navigate the treacherous waters of the End Time is by personal relationship with Jesus and clinging to the hand offered by His Spirit. The Word of God provides direction for day-to-day living in the End Time. Do not be deceived by any source that says otherwise.

The division between those who live by the spirit and those who live by the flesh widens every day. You can't ride two horses traveling in opposite directions. Friends and family members that you pray for every day are moving one way or the other. In this End Time maintaining the status quo is not an option. Feet will move either toward God or away from God.

Forbidden Fruit and the End Time

The end of mankind's story was written as soon as it began in the Garden. The instant Adam's teeth pierced the flesh of the fruit of the Tree of Knowledge of Good and Evil the die was cast. In the book of human history we are nearing the end of the final chapter.

"Then shall they call upon me, but I will not answer; they shall seek me early, but they shall not find me: For that they hated knowledge, and did not choose the fear of the LORD: They would none of my counsel: they despised all my reproof. Therefore shall they eat of the fruit of their own way, and be filled with their own devices." - Proverbs 1:28-31

[63]

The decision Adam and Eve made to eat of the forbidden fruit marked the first of innumerable occasions where humans rejected God's plan in favor of their own. Since Adam and Eve left paradise God not only stretched out His hand but He offered His only Son to die on Calvary's tree in our place - and still no one regards. The opportunity to respond to His call and yield to His plan is yours today.

When is it too late to change your mind? I don't know and neither does anyone else. Many times throughout the course of your life you will discover forbidden fruit in your hand. The face and nature of temptation is unique to each individual. Any idol, addiction, or lust is forbidden fruit. Anything you "just gotta have no matter what" is forbidden fruit unless your only desire is for communion with God.

Does that mean that any sin of idolatry, addiction, or lust is unforgiveable? Certainly not. Your salvation is from such spoiled fruit. The fruit of each new creation in Christ is sweet. Working out your salvation is the exercise of pruning all the poor fruit from your spiritual and physical tree. But there will come one singular moment of decision.

Like every other person, you will have a moment (or moments) when the fruit of temptation is poised at your lips. You may pick up the fruit many times and consider taking a bite but stop short. If the day arrives and you actually pierce its skin and taste of its juice your decision will be made for all eternity.

The Holy Spirit will make known that moment to each child of God; that moment when he or she consciously rejects the forbidden fruit for all time, returns it to God, and commits to never picking it up again.

Have you had this moment? Can you identify the time when you knew it was time to put down the apple and truly deny the world and your human ego in exchange for the supernatural blessing of life with Christ? Unless you are born anew as a creature spiritually joined with God it will be impossible to recognize the forbidden fruit and equally impossible to have the opportunity and spiritual power to reject it.

The forbidden fruit that tempts men and women today is not the same as the actual product of the Garden's central tree; the temptation today is the lie that places humanity and personal opinion over God.

"Because I have called and you refused,
I have stretched out my hand and no one regarded,
Because you disdained all my counsel,
And would have none of my rebuke,
I also will laugh at your calamity;
I will mock when your terror comes,
When your terror comes like a storm,
And your destruction comes like a whirlwind,
When distress and anguish come upon you." - Proverbs 1:24-27

When distilled to its essence, every choice in the world is the one between God and Not God. How you spend your time, your money, and your energy testifies to which choice you made. What education your children receive reflects your choice. Choosing to pursue what you "just gotta have" is choosing the indulgence of one moment over eternity. Choosing Not God is death.

One day your choice will be sealed forever. Today may be that day.

[65]

Rapture-Future and Rapture-Present

"Behold, I tell you a mystery: We shall not all sleep, but we shall all be changed— in a moment, in the twinkling of an eye, at the last trumpet. For the trumpet will sound, and the dead will be raised incorruptible, and we shall be changed". - 1 Corinthians 15:51-52

Turn, O backsliding children, saith the LORD ...and I will take you one of a city, and two of a family, and I will bring you to Zion." - Jeremiah 3:14

Rapture. Without doubt time grows shorter than ever until Christ returns.

The world was corrupted the moment Adam and Eve sinned. Nations, societies, communities, denominations, and families have fallen into the corruption that is the stuff of the world. The heart of Paul's message to the church in Corinth - and all who have gained entrance into the body of Christ since the day it was penned - is that Rapture will occur in an instant and may be one of the most exclusive events in human history.

Earthly Rapture

There is another rapture possible for Christians; one that is available to you today, this minute. There is no preacher, writer, or speaker who can give you the inexpressible joy of such rapture. The questions and discussion in *Rapture and Revelation* have a two-fold purpose: (1) To prepare you for the event that will end your mortal life and (2) To open the door to rapture present.

[67]

Only Jesus Christ makes either rapture possible. None other. If you already know Jesus so intimately that worry, fear, and despair are nothing more than memories, then you already participate in rapture-present that is available for every New Creation in Christ today.

Do you have peace that passes all worldly understanding? Do you have joy every day regardless of economic, physical, or family challenges? Does your spirit sing a new song in praise of Christ, rejoicing even when friends and family reject you?

The goal of *Rapture and Revelation* is to help you measure and compare all that you know and believe against the truth of God's Word as it is written in the Bible and revealed by the Holy Spirit. You will not live in rapture-present, where faith in Christ has extinguished fear, free of anxiety and worry, until you resolve the question, "Why do you believe what you believe?"

Truth is not convenient. Truth does not allow anyone to retain ownership of anything apart from Christ. Truth isn't fancy words or a concept so complex that only religious scholars can master it. Truth is truth. Truth is Jesus Christ, and Him crucified.

An important message of *Rapture and Revelation is:* Don't assume. Don't settle. Don't be led except by the Spirit of God. As new creations in Jesus Christ you can live with rapture presently even while looking forward to Rapture itself.

Are you Rapture Ready?

I have no idea how many will be raptured. The Bible suggests there will be few. How many did God save from the flood when He destroyed the world the first time? There were only eight. God does not care what your church and friends think of you and His kingdom is not a democracy. The determination of whether or not you are ready will not be made by any mortal.

The tether that prevents anyone from joining Christ is the product of their own choices. What is the most fundamental choice? God or Not God. How do you know if you've made the right choices, that you followed the right path, and that you are ready to hear your Savior call?

It is only possible to choose wisely when you have the correct facts. False-teachers and prophets have been working their mischief for centuries. Many, if not most, of the major denominations have been leading their members away from the path leading to the Narrow Gate. [Matthew 7:13]

Who would have believed that gays would marry, that babies would be conceived in laboratories but murdered in clinics, and that Jesus would become just some guy who loves everybody like some 1960's Hippie guru preaching "Free love"? There is no free love found in the Bible. God loves us, and the price of His love was the blood of His only Son.

Do you know the Ten Commandments? How many have you broken in the past year? Do you honor the Sabbath day and keep it holy?

Do you have anything in your home that God would object to? Books, magazines, movies, or other art? What about your children?

Do you give your first and your best to the Lord each day? Every day?

Are entertainments, sports, music, art, dance, or competitions more important than fellowship with others in the body of Christ? Do you forego church assembly or Bible study to watch your grandchild play soccer?

How many hours a week do you devote to the important relationships in your life?

- Spouse
- Children
- Parents
- Friends
- Television
- Surfing the Web
- Gaming
- Church
- Volunteering
- Hobbies
- Sports
- Shopping
- Stewardship of home and property

What makes you believe you are Rapture ready? Are you already living in rapture-present? Do you spend sufficient time with your children every day? The proof is in the fruit. Are they balanced, confident, obedient, prayerful, generous, and successful in the things of childhood?

Has your relationship with your spouse deepened and strengthened since your last anniversary? Do you pray together daily? Are you a workaholic? Alcoholic? Shopaholic?

The quality of your relationships and your use of time, energy, treasure, and emotion is proof of your choice between God and Not God.

How many hours each week remain for relationship with God? *What* do you believe and *why* do you believe it? What is at stake? Everything.

[70]

Using Logic to Examine the Existence and Effect of God

"Plato understood that you have to have absolutes, or nothing has meaning."

"It is not a chaotic world. If that were true that all is chaotic, unrelated, and absurd, science as well as general life would come to an end." - Dr. Frances Schaeffer, *He Is There and He Is Not Silent*, pp. 280, 286

If the God of the Bible exists then He is the creator of all that is and the One who establishes every absolute. What He says is true is true and the opposite must then be false.

If the God of the Bible exists then the Bible itself must be absolutely true. If part of it is false then the whole is worthless no matter if some truth is hidden among the errors like *The DaVinci Code* and *The Shack*. The Bible is either absolutely true or it is not.

If God exists and the Bible is absolutely true then the only absolute standard is God's standard. Humans may come up with their own set of rules and policies but no regulation or legislated mandate will ever change whether something is or is not true.

Recently some courts have ruled that if a person born male wishes to live as a female and be considered a female, then that person will, by law, be considered a female. The same is true for a female who desires to be a male and, by judicial signature, becomes one.

Progressive thinkers may believe they have human kindness at heart, but that kindness is based on a lie. The biological sex of an

[71]

individual cannot be changed by the signature of an elected or appointed human or even by the hands of a skilled surgeon.

If it weren't so tragic, such decisions to modify gender would be laughable. It is theoretically possible in such circumstances for a woman to become a man on Monday and change back to a woman on Friday, just because he/she wants to. All that's needed is a sworn statement of desire and perhaps a counselor to sign off on it.

Before the first gender change and after the second, that person will still genetically be either a male or a female. That cannot be changed. All you can alter is appearance and what you call such a person.

Science can't exist without God

The foundation of science is the process of experimentation based upon the Scientific Method. To prove causality the Scientific Method allows only one variable to be changed at a time so that any change in results may be rightly attributed to whatever variable was changed. The basic belief is that all other factors not being changed will remain constant.

A simple illustration would be two identical glasses of water. The experiment uses two of the same glasses, the same water, and the same amount of water in each glass. The only thing different is that one of the glasses is placed into a freezer and the other is not.

The water in the glass in the freezer gets hard and is transformed into ice. Using the Scientific Method we rightly conclude that the reason the water turned into ice was the freezer because everything else about the two glasses of water was identical.

If science could not assume that non-variables remain constant the experimental process would be useless. In other words, if you couldn't safely assume that the water wouldn't just change by happenstance then you couldn't say for sure that the freezer caused the water in one glass to become ice.

What about the theory that battles the Creation story of Genesis? Every scientific theory that denies Creation depends upon chance and the passage of time to explain how nothing became something. Scientists and any other people who object to Creation are denying the very principle that makes science work - the concept of constants or absolutes. There had to be some variable that resulted in each step of Creation. The only possible variable is God.

If everything is random we're all insane

Albert Einstein once described insanity as doing the same thing but expecting a different result. No living creature can exist in a state of total randomness. Out of chaos God created order.

Animals subject to experiments where punishment has no connection to behavior eventually lose their sanity. Neurosis is the step before insanity where the brain enters a sort of self-defense mode. Neurosis is often the result of partial randomness, where there is some relationship between what we do in our world and what the world does with us, but not reliably so.

Imagine that you are being tortured with painful shocks applied randomly - without rhyme or reason. You have no power to predict or change the outcome. Eventually your mind will simply shut down, become catatonic, or go completely insane.

God provides order, security, boundaries, and absolutes that produce solid building blocks for life, society, and relationship with Him. When you hear scientists talk about random events, remember this link between randomness and insanity.

Abortion Rights Activists Deny Logic

According to worldly wisdom an unborn child is a person or a lump of disposable flesh depending upon the whim of a woman with the right to choose.

There are many in the United States that consider the right to abortion as one of the most important in life. They believe this right to choose is part of the Constitutional protection of their right to life, liberty, and the pursuit of happiness.

If absolutes exist then the fetus must always be a baby or always be a lump of disposable flesh. Since human mothers have never delivered anything other than a human baby it would be a hard sell to convince people that their grandchildren are nothing more than genetic trash.

That gets us back to where we started. Progressives believe that your god can be anything you want as long as mine can be whatever I want. The truth is there is only one way for any god to be meaningful, and that is if that god is the God of the Bible.

Many argue that Christianity is an illogical and unhealthy crutch for people who deny reality and science. On the contrary, without the God who exists, the God of the Bible, there could be no science.

If God exists, then His is the absolute supreme authority. What He makes true is always true regardless of whether any human agrees or disagrees. Does the sun rise in the east? Would you bet your life on whether it will do the same tomorrow? Why are you so sure?

[74]

Rapture - The First Wave

Will all who confess Christ as the Son of God and their personal Savior take up residence in the mansion promised in John 14:2? Absolutely, because the Bible is true.

There are some Christians who don't believe in the concept of Rapture. I don't intend to argue with them. But there are a couple of questions that occurred to me and if these questions have an answer that squares with the Bible there almost has to be a rapture.

What I am about to suggest is based upon the Bible but does not come directly from the Bible. Please rely upon your own understanding and relationship with Jesus as you consider these two questions;

1. "Can any other person take your salvation from you?"

2. "What is the purpose for evangelism and ministry - or for writing this book?"

"He chose us in Him before the foundation of the world, that we should be holy and without blame before Him in love, having predestined us to adoption as sons by Jesus Christ to Himself." - Ephesians 1:4-5

God knew all who would be His before the beginning of the world. If that is so, then the names in the Lamb's Book of Life are written with indelible ink.

There is no question about the destiny of each one whose name was covered in the spilled blood of Christ. Jesus Christ knew the name of

[75]

each person He died for on the Cross. The list was there and his precious blood covered every name that appeared on the list at the foot of the Cross when He cried, "It is finished."

On that specific date and at that specific hour the content of the Lamb's Book of Life was completed. If your name was on that list you are guaranteed arrival in the mansion prepared especially for you. Because God's time cannot be fathomed by mortals, all we can do is admit that God lives in the eternal "Now" and that what was is yet to be, and what is yet to be has already been.

If there is a sure guarantee of salvation by predestination then why are we called to evangelize and preach the gospel? One reason must certainly be obedience; doing as God asks. But if our mansion is guaranteed, is anything really at stake if we choose not to obey? Is anything truly at risk?

As we move on, please consider this next question carefully and prayerfully; does your salvation depend upon the action or inaction of any other human on earth today?

Can my lack of obedience to carry a message change your eternal outcome? If I fail to take a message to New Zealand does that mean it is possible for someone there to end up in the lake of fire because of my failure? The answer is, "No!" Jesus' payment of our debt was complete and sufficient. My salvation does not depend on you and yours is not dependent upon what anyone else does or does not do.

If the process of carrying a message - evangelizing - is not material to the salvation of another person, how is it important at all? If God has called you to any particular task or ministry it is certainly very relevant to your own relationship with God. Whatever you do in either obedience or disobedience to the call God has given you is material *to you* and to the issue of your life in rapture-present.

[76]

Certainly God uses us as His hands, feet, and workers to accomplish His will. However, if you decide you don't want to accept a call to teach, preach, or serve in missions, God will select another to take your place. Your refusal will not blot out any name from the Book of Life.

What is the real purpose of evangelizing or ministry?

What might the ultimate purpose for evangelism, ministry, and writing this book be? If the salvation of one person does not depend on the actions or inaction of someone else, why do we keep trying - other than sheer obedience?

There is no verse to be cited since this is but a rhetorical question that begs an answer. Writing *Rapture and Revelation* is certainly an act of obedience for me, but is there a larger purpose? Is there actually something at stake?

Is the work of ministry really nothing more than spiritual busy work? My answer is *no*. God wastes nothing. He uses every good thing and every bad thing for the benefit of His children who love Him. [Romans 8:28]

The message you bring to another person may equip him or her to confess Christ, choose God, and to be in fellowship with the church soon to be raptured by Christ. Refusing to share your testimony with others will not cost them their salvation, but you may prevent them from finding their place at Rapture. Your disobedience may also result in being left behind yourself with plenty of time to consider your error.

Being left behind in the Rapture does not mean you will not be saved and that you will lose the promise of eternity with Christ. What *may* be at stake, however, is the timing and manner of your journey home.

As I worked through this line of inquiry I considered how our actions might be relevant in some different way to the salvation of others due to the nature of God's time. Since He lives in the Eternal Now, could my testimony actually be needed to ensure the salvation of someone else?

Then I came right back around to the beginning. No one's salvation depends on anything other than the finished work of Jesus Christ. Sure, God may know exactly who each of us will speak to throughout our lives and what we'll say, but nothing I do will either save or condemn anyone else.

Will all who confess Christ as the Son of God be raptured? No. Christ told us that many who speak and do wonders in His name will discover at the most unfortunate time that He never knew them. [Matthew 7:23]

Speaking a few simple words or having some errant belief in god, jesus, or grace is not sufficient. You must be participating in a committed personal relationship with Jesus Christ himself and be indwelt by His Holy Spirit to receive the unmerited Grace His death provided.

Rapture Relationship and Christian Standards

What is the standard for Christians who pursue a right relationship with Christ? The standard presented in 2 Corinthians 5:15 deals with the choice you made between living for yourself and living for Christ.

Christians delude themselves in much the same way as non-Christians. Would you be surprised to learn that 72% of Americans believe that they can disagree with what their religion teaches on abortion and "still be considered a person of good standing in their faith"? [Public Religion Research Institute study, 2011] In other words, people believe they may set their own standards for faith without consequence. When the standards you choose to reject are God's standards, you place yourself in a very precarious and foolish position.

Christians who meet His standard will be in the first wave of redemption, or what is generally known as the Rapture. How can you meet such lofty standards? It's not humanly possible, is it?

"But Jesus looked at them and said to them, "With men this is impossible, but with God all things are possible." - Matthew 19:26

It is not possible for a human to meet God's standard. The good news for you as a new creation in Jesus Christ is that the power of the Holy Spirit can elevate you beyond what is humanly possible. Working through God's Word we find that there may be a difference between being saved and being Rapture ready.

As an ambassador of God, Paul implored those who would listen to be reconciled to God. Today you are being called to listen and to reconcile yourself to God through relationship with His Son. There are no acceptable mitigating conditions or excuses, no matter what you hear from "trusted" non-biblical sources. God does not grade on the curve and each one of us will be held to the same standard of living preached in the 1st century.

Whose Praise do you Love More?

Many false teachers in the world today assure both the gullible and vulnerable that all they need do is believe in Jesus Christ and they

[79]

will be saved. Such assurances get bodies into the church, but such promises are empty and will not get the 'believer' into heaven.

Simple belief is not synonymous with commitment. I may believe that eating liver is good for me but I don't intend to let one bite of the stuff make its way onto my fork. Liver is simply not to my taste. Satan believes in Jesus Christ, but he will never make a commitment to Christ.

Jesus had a full schedule and an exciting week as the days ticked down before the Last Supper and His arrest. He dined with Lazarus, Mary and Martha in Bethany; He rode the unbroken colt during His triumphant entry into Jerusalem welcomed by shouts of Hosanna and a carpet of palm branches.

During that week Jesus also taught the people. Though many did not accept Him as the Messiah, even some of the Pharisees became believers. Although these religious rulers believed Jesus to be the Christ, they still refused to confess Him lest they be "put out of the synagogue, for they loved the praise of men more than the praise of God." [John 12:42-43]

The Pharisees stood in the very company of the man, Jesus. Even though they believed that He was the Messiah they chose the world of men over the Son of God. For that they will be condemned. It's not difficult for reasonable people to understand and agree that the Pharisees deserve what they have coming.

Mere belief in Jesus Christ has no power to save, let alone to grant passage in Rapture. Such teachings are simply not true. First one believes, then one confesses, then one's new nature in Christ begets a visible change in how he lives and how he behaves. Satan believes in Jesus, but he won't be in attendance at the wedding feast when Christ and His Bride celebrate their marriage.

[80]

Belief is a requirement for salvation but is not the only requirement. [John 3:7] Are you a New Creation? [2 Corinthians 5:17] Have you really changed from what you were into something different? Does the praise of God mean more to you than earthly accolades from *anyone*? Do you possess a peace that passes understanding and joy that banishes fear? [John 14:27]

What you believe is important. But equally important to what you believe is knowing *why* you believe it.

Rapture: Theory and Requirement

"The rapture is something to strive for, a worthiness we hope for, a reward we do not presume to have attained, but a prize." Bible verses that speak to Rapture *"do not distinguish between believers and the wicked, but between faithful believers and not so worthy believers."* - Jason Hommel, Bibleprophesy.org

There is a lack of consensus among theologians and believers on the fact of the Rapture as well as the timing of the Rapture. Will the church be raptured to live in eternity with Christ (1) before the great Tribulation, (2) at the three-and-a-half-year mid-point, or (3) at the end of the Tribulation?

No one can say with certainty when we shall be called to meet Jesus in the air since the Bible does not specifically say. The most important point to remember is that regardless of which theory is correct (if any) Jesus Christ has redeemed you and you will occupy the mansion He promised. [John 14:2]

My personal belief is that the church of Christ will be raptured before the Tribulation. If you are curious about the minor theories of mid-Tribulation or post-Tribulation Rapture you can find information at the library, online, or by asking your pastor.

There is little doubt that we are moving ahead with increasing speed toward the day of Rapture. Don't you wonder just how much of depravity, lies, and evil the church of Christ will have to endure before being called home? Most biblical scholars agree that there is no element of Bible prophecy yet to be accomplished before the End Time transitions into Tribulation except for the Rapture.

[83]

The body of Christ is being hunted by the soldiers of Satan. It's that simple. Any child of the King who looks upward and ahead to joining Jesus in the air at Rapture is prey to the evil one and his minions.

Jesus tells us what to expect in these verses:

"And you will be hated by all for My name's sake. But he who endures to the end will be saved. When they persecute you in this city, flee to another. For assuredly, I say to you, you will not have gone through the cities of Israel before the Son of Man comes." - Matthew 10:22-23

Will everyone saved be raptured? I don't think so. The book of Revelation provides ample evidence of new converts to Christ during the Tribulation as well as the refining of those who already confessed Christ but were unprepared to fly when Christ called the church to meet Him in the air.

"And he said to me, These are they which came out of great tribulation, and have washed their robes, and made them white in the blood of the Lamb." - Revelation 7:14

What is at stake for every Christian in this End Time is the manner and timing of his departure from the world. Will you do all you can to be in right relationship with Christ so that you will be safe above when the Tribulation begins?

The Gate is Narrow and the Path Hidden

Jesus makes it clear that the gate to eternal life is narrow, the path difficult, and that precious few will find it. [Matthew 7: 14] Have you ever stopped to consider just how narrow that gate might be and difficult it may really be to find? Most folks make the easy assumption that just because they go to church or call themselves

[84]

christian they will enjoy door-to-door valet service and be deposited directly in front of heaven's entrance gate when their time comes.

Cheap grace is the lie that says the way will be made clear for everyone. Cheap grace insinuates that new birth is not required for salvation. Cheap grace declares that communion with the Spirit of God is not necessary for passage through the narrow gate. Cheap grace sweeps aside the need for repentance of sin to live in eternity with a holy God. Cheap grace preaches that the concept of sin is old-fashioned and unworthy of today's highly evolved men and women.

Cheap grace is not the Grace of God. Cheap grace proves the old adage that you get what you pay for and cheap grace has no value.

Many of today's Christians hope they'll find the path to that narrow gate and squeeze through like Santa Claus down a six-inch wide chimney on December 24th. That whole Santa Claus deal is a myth. Are you willing to bet your life that hope based on cheap grace isn't just as fanciful?

The difficult path and narrow gate describe limiting factors that sift the found from the lost, and those prepared to be raptured from those who are not. Half of the virgins awaiting the bridegroom ran out of oil for their lamps. They were unprepared. In this parable half missed their opportunity to be part of the wedding feast. When they cried for late admittance they were told they were nothing more than strangers. [Matthew 25:1-12]

Why might the Rapture be one of the most exclusive events in human history? Only eight souls survived the flood.[Genesis 7:13] If Sodom had even ten righteous people in the entire population it would have been spared from total annihilation. [Genesis 18:32] Ten righteous were not found and you know how that story ended.

[85]

It seems clear that a similar message is appropriate for the body of Christ today. There is only one key that unlocks the narrow gate to heaven. Not only must you know the key to the gate, but what is most important is that the Key [Christ] knows who you are.

"Many will say to me in that day, Lord, Lord, have we not prophesied in thy name? And in thy name have cast out devils? And in thy name done many wonderful works? Only those who do the will of God will enter heaven. And then will I profess unto them, I never knew you: depart from me, ye that work iniquity."
- Matthew 7:21-23

Only the passionate daily pursuit of right relationship with Jesus Christ will show you the way to the path, see you safely along the way, and open the gate wide enough for you to pass through unhindered. Who is responsible for getting your feet on the right path? You are; not any pastor, priest, author, evangelist, spouse, or scholar.

Playing chicken with the line separating what is righteous from what is not is a good way to crash and burn. Are you positive you are on the right side of that line?

Establishing the Line between Right and Wrong

Who sets the line that divides right from wrong? I suggest that this is the work of the Holy Spirit. If you ask 100 people to outline the limits placed upon behavior by the 10 Commandments you will get many different answers. How many of those answers will be correct?

Again, every parent with more than one child has a unique relationship with each one. The same is true of the relationship between God our Father and each Christian. Different kids have different temptations and challenges. Some kids are naturally busy. They're always looking for the next challenge. Some kids are

[86]

motivated to solve problems and undertake challenges just for the fun of finding the solution or winning a mental or physical contest.

Some children just want to get along. They are content to be couch potatoes and the opportunity to win something won't motivate them enough to get them to even read the rules. Some children are natural pleasers while others crave the next battle. One child in a family may have a particularly tender heart while another is a drama queen made of ice. The rules that work best for raising children must be drawn based upon their unique personalities, temptations, attributes, and needs.

While the type and style of relationships vary greatly, does God recognize more than one *definition* of right relationship? I don't think so. What about behavior? Is it probable that God allows for different interpretations of right behavior among his vastly different children? There are absolute requirements regarding right relationship with God and righteous behavior that are unchangeable and not open for debate. But once those foundational truths are established you move into the area of disputable things.

To whom much is given much is required

God showers blessings on us each day. Does that mean that the pathway narrows each time you receive another relational gift? The immediate answer is, "Yes." These questions apply to me personally as well as those called to lead, to minister, or to carry a message to the body of Christ. There is a higher standard. A particular behavior that lies on the right side of the line for one person may be on the wrong side for leaders, teachers, and pastors.

The Bible cautions us to not teach what we have not yet mastered. Anyone who accepts a teaching role must accept the authority and accountability that raises the bar of right behavior. Pastors will be held accountable for doctrinal or behavioral lapses that might be tolerated from a lay teacher or congregant. [Luke 12:48]

Parents are held to a higher standard than their children. Teachers are held to a higher standard than their students. Generals are held to a higher standard than corporals. The treasurer entrusted with the purse is held to a higher standard than one who contributes.

Frequently striking the wrong keys on a piano may be completely acceptable when done by a pianist who gamely volunteers to play for worship services. Those brave souls deserve the gratitude of their fellows. On the other hand, you will expect far more from a highly skilled (and paid) organist and you will be far less forgiving of repeated errors.

No one is perfect. Each time someone steps up or steps out front in a teaching or leadership role a new level of behavior should be required of that individual; one that exceeds the burden borne by those being led or educated. In return they have a right to expect the support and regard of those they serve in addition to respect, concern, prayer, and love. [1 Thessalonians 5:12-13]

What is the requirement for being Rapture Ready?

The only impediment to being Rapture-ready is your own unwillingness. This is a difficult concept to grasp, because who wouldn't be willing to be raptured and escape the earthly horror to follow?

Everyone wants to be a millionaire, but not everyone is willing to do what must be done to achieve that lofty goal. Many people think it would be nice to have an advanced academic degree but they aren't willing to do the work required to fill out an application to graduate school, much less complete the coursework for graduation.

The most common resolution made every New Year's Eve is to lose weight and exercise more. Most of these resolutions are broken and forgotten by Valentine's Day. In such cases there was an unwillingness to make the commitment needed on January 2nd and beyond to accomplish the goal.

Any human called to relationship with Jesus Christ by the Spirit of God is *able* to become ready for Rapture. The finished work of Christ on Calvary makes us able. Like the wannabe's of wealth, education, and physical fitness, most people are just not willing to do what must be done to achieve success.

There are some who disagree with me, saying that God is too loving to exclude people from experiencing Rapture because of such unfair and difficult standards. The reason for the dispute is the belief that humans are sinners and simply cannot to meet the requirements. This is another lie of cheap grace. Humans certainly can meet the very narrow and strict standard of behavior required for Rapture. What makes you able, and this miracle possible, is the Holy Spirit that transforms your "old man" into the new creation in Christ Jesus you are today. [Matthew 19:25-26]

There is no lack of ability to walk in right relationship with Jesus that the Holy Spirit cannot repair. There is no inability, no impediment to salvation, no lack of ability or understanding that God cannot or will not overcome. While it is true that God makes all able, He requires each of us to be willing. God will never *make* us do anything.

All error is not sin

Jesus instructs us to "go and sin no more." [John 5:14, John 8:11] We have no excuse for repeating the same sin over and over knowing in advance that our thought or behavior is a sin. Once sin

[89]

has been brought to your attention by the Holy Spirit you may be forgiven of it by repenting of that specifically named sin. Any decision to repeat that same confessed sin brings with it a conviction of purposeful premeditation.

There is no blanket forgiveness for daily sin. If your habit is to spend the last moment before sleep praying for forgiveness of "anything I did today" then you're barking up the wrong tree. God can't (or won't) deal with fill-in-the-blank confession of sin. There is no learning, no growth, and no increase in faith possible by forgiveness of unnamed sin.

How would you respond if your spouse asked for forgiveness each night from any and all unfaithfulness he or she committed during the day? Wouldn't the first thing out of your mouth be, "And what unfaithfulness do I need to know about?"

You vowed to be faithful to your spouse. If you're not sure what that means, ask your wife or husband. I'm sure there will be plenty to talk over. When you accepted Christ as your personal Savior you became a new creation. Your commitment to Christ is no less specific than the one you made on your wedding day. Indeed, you are the Bride of Christ and He expects you to be faithful.

Sin is cheating. Sin is adultery. Sin is lust. Your spouse is probably eager to discuss what he or she considers cheating, adultery, or lust. The Bible and the Holy Spirit are equally available and committed to discussing the difference between a sin and a mistake. All you need do is ask.

Mistakes happen all the time. All error is not sin. Perfection in any form is simply not possible for mortals. There is an evolution of faith within each new creation. The longer you walk with Christ the less likely you are to sin. That does not mean that you won't make mistakes. You may never get past making plenty of unintended errors, but God expects you to sin less and less as your journey together progresses.

Mistakes are not sin. Sin is sin. The Bible speaks to sin, not to mistakes.

God makes you Able but will not make you Willing

One unresolved issue frequently raised by Christians concerns the salvation of unborn children as well as children and adults without the mental capacity to make reasoned decisions about faith. The same problem arises with populations who are in remote places of the world without access to missionaries or media evangelists.

The concern is, "What about them?" What happens to souls such as these?

In every case the question arises because the person is not *unwilling* to make a rational choice but is *unable* to choose. An aborted child cannot choose God. The child with a severe learning disability may be prevented from understanding what Christ offers. And how can people who never hear the gospel message choose Christ?

Once you recognize that there is no lack of willingness on the part of any person described here the only possibility that remains is that they *could not* commit to life with Christ because they were unable.

There are only two simple reasons why a relationship or goal fails - the person is either unable or unwilling to succeed. Since it is not possible for a miscarried or aborted baby to be unwilling to consider Christ the only choice left is a lack of ability; an obstacle God will be faithful to remove.

The Gospel Message - Hearing vs Receiving

If a person has truly never heard the gospel message then it was not possible for him or her to refuse Christ. Such a one is unable, not unwilling. *Hearing* the gospel message is not necessarily the same as *receiving* the gospel message. How many people read the Bible, attend a church service, participate in a discussion with friends or family and not "hear" the gospel message? How many of you responded completely the very first time you realized that a man named Jesus lived and that He died to save sinners?

Most Christians weren't born again as new creations in Christ the very first time they heard the salvation message. The point is that refusing to respond to the message is not the same as never hearing the message. You heard the words of the message; you just didn't hear it with your spirit tuned to the right frequency before. You heard the message, you just did not accept the message.

"Entitlements" of Satan vs. Unmerited Blessings from God

The voice of the Enemy speaks through the failed leadership of parents, pastors, politicians, and teachers when they speak lies about entitlement to children and adults alike. There is no respect for authority and precious few, if any, consequences for bad choices made at home, in school, in the workplace, on Main Street, and in the churches.

God forgives, absolves, and overcomes every inability. No sheep will ever be lost in the wilderness because it *could not* return to the fold. If a sheep from Christ's flock is trapped in a pit too deep to crawl out of or is too far from home for its cries to be heard, God will be faithful to create any circumstance necessary to rescue that lost one. The finished work of Jesus Christ is a sure guarantee that every lost, trapped, or desperate sheep will be able to return home.

On the other hand, God cannot and will not overlook the unwillingness of a sheep to come when the Shepherd calls. Every sheep that hears the voice crying out for it to return, yet refuses to start walking will be left in the wilderness. What the voice of the unwilling sheep says to God is, "No, I won't!"

Do you really think He will respond, "Oh, never mind, I'll come out and drag you in"? God is an almighty God, a Holy God, and the only God. God will not go out to bring in any rebellious sheep that stomps its little hoof and challenges Him to, "Make me!"

People believe they are entitled to food, shelter, entertainment, and education for no other reason than that they are human. People of faith add one more item to that long list of entitlements - salvation. Some pastors teach that nothing is needed for salvation other than being made in the image of God.

There are three ways to receive unmerited blessing, (1) as a gift of grace, (2) as a gift of love, or (3) as a gift of charity. This is true whether the blessing in question is granted to man by God or from one human (or organization) to another. Entitlements have become major players in our nation through government programs. Benefits given to those who have done nothing to deserve them are unmerited. The very term "entitlement" is the work of the Enemy and has corrupted the government, the people, and the church of Jesus Christ.

The only blessings to which we are entitled are those promised by God Himself. The Pilgrims didn't invent the requirement that one must work in order to eat. It isn't some political philosophy or discrimination that denies unearned blessing -- it is the Word of God. [2 Thessalonians 3:10]

If all that is needed to receive God's grace and promise of eternal life is being human then the remainder of the Bible is a lie. Only human arrogance assumes such a lofty place in God's estimation. And, like most assumptions, it is wrong. Humanists teach that men and women are equal to God. Satan is working hard to sell the message that God needs to be brought down to mortal level.

The message of the Bible is that we may one day be elevated to God's presence through the sacrifice of Jesus which offers unmerited grace to believers. That elevation will only be complete in a glorified and immortal body and not the one you're walking around in today.

Anything that suggests that God and humans are in any way equal is of the Enemy. Humanists believe in the deity of mankind. But what possible value could there be in a completely human god? When humans attribute a character and nature to God that is equal to their own He is transformed from God to god; stripped of truth, deity, and any real ability to save. God shared part of His character with us. The arrogance of an opposite philosophy paves the path to Hell.

Any god who shares the least common denominator with a human is no god at all.

The unmerited blessings of government and others are either gifts or lies. The concept of entitlement is the work of Satan. An entitlement is something required by contract based upon equal sides. If you agree to sell me an apple for a dollar I am entitled to the apple and you are entitled to the dollar.

Anything given without an equal payment of labor or value is a gift. Much of the debt problem in both our national economy and the faith community comes from calling a gift an entitlement. No person deserves free meals, free money, or free anything simply because he or she is human. The lie that changed a gift of love or charity into an entitlement transformed the gift itself from a blessing into a curse.

Christians who believe that folks are entitled to support simply because they breathe will also believe the lie that everyone will enter heaven. God never said so. The author of that lie is Satan.

What do you believe? Why?

Rapture - Relationship - Rationalization

Many people think that religion has a place in their life and that is should be kept in that place and not allowed out except on Sunday. I've had people tell me they really appreciate my writing about training horses, but would I please keep the Bible out of the barn? Such criticism is usually prefaced with the words, "I am a Christian, but…"

Do you separate decisions made in your daily life from Scripture because you think it is possible to compartmentalize different aspects of life? Do you believe that one part of your life may truly be separated from any other? When you decide to seal off any part of your life with a "Do Not Enter" sign the Spirit will not trespass. Any part of your body, your life, or your personality you decide to keep apart from the Holy Spirit remains outside of His power. He respects every boundary established by your free will.

God will respect your space. If you don't allow God to rule in the smallest areas of your life, why would you expect Him to appear when you need supernatural power?

What do you think about little white lies? Do you watch any television programs that God might frown upon? Does the Word of God go into the voting booth with you?

Separating any part of your body, or element of your life, from God, is by definition a choice to sin. Compartmentalizing removes God from whatever you keep for yourself. There is no other reason to separate except to continue to sin. When people engage in any lust they separate their body and that part of their life from God. That

[97]

decision means they are on their own in that arena and good luck to them.

Rapture Roulette

Most Christians today are engaged in a very dangerous game I call Rapture Roulette.

Russian Roulette is a stupid game where one bullet is loaded into a six-shot revolver. The players sit in a circle and pass the gun from one to the next. Taking a turn means spinning the cylinder so there is a 1 in 6 chance of the bullet firing when the player points the gun at his head and squeezes the trigger. If you live you pass the gun to the next idiot who spins the chamber and takes a gamble on committing suicide.

Rapture Roulette is also a stupid game of chance preached by false teachers as sound Christian doctrine. Players in Rapture Roulette bet that they will be Rapture-ready as long as they aren't sinning at the very moment Christ calls.

Rapture Roulette rules state that if you cheated on your spouse yesterday but feel bad about it today your day-old sin doesn't count. Rapture Roulette players bet that Jesus will forgive every sin because they were told He would.

Rapture Roulette players believe that the odds of taking the bullet are slim. Are you willing to take that gamble or will you seek out the sure and certain promise of Jesus Christ? He is the Shepherd of obedient sheep, not the ones who challenge him to "Make me" and choose to continue in their sin.

Sin is a shackle by which we are chained to the world. The chain is of our own making.

[98]

Departure Delayed - Compartmentalization

God asks us for complete relationship. Becoming a new creation always creates a change in behavior from what you used to do to what you do today. Are we works in progress? Certainly.

Every new creation has blind spots where sin or error is committed without understanding. Fellowship and accountability within a community of believers is one way you find out where your blemishes remain. The other is to allow the Holy Spirit to illuminate every corner of your spirit until all the dirt and filth have been exposed and swept away.

Do we sin? Yes. Will God's grace pardon that sin? Yes, as long as the sin is the result of ignorance and not willful rebellion against God.

Can you imagine Jesus translating you out of this world when you are deep in sin at the very moment He comes? When you knowingly commit a sin or refuse to lay down every part of your life to Christ you will be left behind. No one knows the day or hour. You may enjoy the prizes of power, lust, or addiction by playing Rapture Roulette, but once the Tribulation begins those treasures will quickly tarnish and sour.

There are consequences to your actions and consequences for the choices you make. And make no mistake; you have all the choice in the world about how to live your life. Of course there are some limitations to what you can do, but the way you live and relate to Jesus Christ is 100% within your control.

Can you really separate your mornings from your evenings, your leisure from your labor, your work from your play, or your daily life from Life with Christ? Where is the point of division? Night and morning always meet and all you do is in the sight of Christ.

Treason - Separate at Your Own Risk

When you indulge in any addiction, whether drugs, alcohol, gluttony, sex, pornography, spiritualism, or gambling - that portion of your life and body are removed from the field of battle and you will fight on your own. God will not allow His Spirit or His angels to wage war on your behalf when you have chosen to ally yourself with the Enemy.

God won't help you if you are unwilling to change and give up the sin that got you in the mess in the first place. The only way the Holy Spirit can clean the mess out of your home or your life is by knocking down the walls you put up trying to keep Him out. Restoration is possible, but only by relationship with Jesus Christ where your repentance results in His forgiveness.

"For what fellowship has righteousness with lawlessness? And what communion has light with darkness?" - 2 Corinthians 6:14

"I will no longer talk much with you, for the ruler of this world is coming, and he has nothing in Me." - John 14:30

What part of treason don't you understand? The Good News of the Gospel is that you may return to His camp by renouncing your allegiance to sin. Jesus Christ provided a pass that allows you to cross back into full relationship with Him. A full and complete relationship with Jesus Christ is only possible when you hold nothing back. The good news of the Gospel is that there is nothing broken He cannot repair.

The Sinner's Prayer

Tele-evangelists and pastors across the globe offer salvation to congregants and first-time visitors alike if they just pray the right words. "Pray this prayer with me and you'll be saved!" Such an offer is not scriptural. There are no magic words that invoke salvation. Such teaching is the stuff of a witch's incantation.

Salvation begins with the admission and repentance of sin, shame, and the realization that we are unable to do anything on our own to gain entrance into heaven. It is only the grace of God through the Cross of Christ that saves. It is only the Spirit of the Living God that makes a new creation of us. Words are appropriate when making a public profession of newfound faith, but words alone have no power to save.

How many vows before "God and this company" have been made between brides and grooms to forsake all others and remain faithful until parted by death? Millions of weddings precede the numerous infidelities that follow. Marriage in most communities requires a license and involves what is often a ridiculous amount of pomp, circumstance, and debt in celebration of a relationship that is guaranteed to end one day by death, divorce, or annulment.

If wedding vows fail in nearly half of all marriages, how realistic is it to assume that the momentary urge to recite a simple prayer will create a relationship divine, supernatural, and eternal? Marriage vows are symbolic and profess publicly that which is written in our heart and spirit. The key to success, however, is the commitment renewed each morning for the rest of the natural life.

Accepting Christ as Lord and Savior by praying in public is much the same. Of themselves the words have no power, but when they represent a complete change of one's spiritual DNA, the power is given by God to become truly and eternally His.

Rationalization and Rapture

Rationalization is the game played by most humans today. People tell themselves lies every day about why it is acceptable to separate some part of their body or life from God's will. His will saves. Their "won't" condemns.

If you are indulging in any known sin you will not be taken up when the Church is raptured because you have willingly chained part of your body or your life to the world. It is impossible to become airborne to meet Jesus with such tethers.

Perhaps playing Rapture Roulette with your salvation won't result in eternal condemnation, but it sure won't let you fly away when Christ calls His church to come home.

Pursue a right relationship with Jesus Christ. Keep nothing separate from His peace, healing, and care and you will be free to join Him at the Rapture. Choose to retain control and autonomy in any aspect of body or life and you will remain on earth to enjoy that which you insisted on withholding from the Spirit.

The choice is yours. If you profess Jesus Christ as your Savior, how can you possibly justify evicting Him from any area of your life? Every thought matters. He knows them all. Every action matters, He sees them all. If Jesus died to pay the debt for all your sins then there is nothing that remains uncovered. But, if you choose to restrict access of His cleansing blood from reaching every part of your life, you have chosen to retain the dark stain of sin in those places you kept the flow from entering.

[102]

No one may stand before God unless he is holy, sinless, and without stain. Your choice to remain blemished bars you from entrance into the presence of God. Sin cannot stand before the throne and Jesus cannot lead you to heaven as a raptured saint when you willingly wear the filth of guilt.

"And Jesus answered and spoke to them again by parables and said: The kingdom of heaven is like a certain king who arranged a marriage for his son, and sent out his servants to call those who were invited to the wedding; and they were not willing to come." - Matthew 22:1-3

Living in the Gateway of the Cross

If you're at least as old as I am you may remember the original 1960's Star Trek television show with William Shatner playing James Tiberius Kirk, captain of the USS Enterprise. Several storylines centered on a portal, a door-like opening in the fabric of time and space that connected one reality with another or as a tear in the time/space barrier that separated one universe composed of matter with an identical universe made of anti-matter.

A portal is the place where different dimensions or planes intersect. If you are on one side all you see is what is there. Transition to the other side and you see a new reality that does not include what you saw on the "other side."

If you watch one of these episodes of Star Trek you might see a camera shot of an actor entering the portal. As the actor's arm and leg moved through the opening they disappeared from sight. The camera shot would then change to one (supposedly) on the other side showing the arm and leg coming into the new reality on the other side.

The Gateway of the Cross is like a supernatural portal where the vertical member of the cross of Jesus Christ intersects with the horizontal member. This opening creates a physical and spiritual place where the Holy Spirit connects our practical and actual earthly state with our life lived in relationship with Christ. This place of collision opens whenever a New Creation in Christ is born.

The Gateway explains how you can be in the world but not of the world. The portal is the place where we see the world around us but may also receive regular glimpses into the next. The other side is populated with angels, spirits, God, and Jesus Christ. The other side, the not-of-this-world crowd, has no difficulty observing our world but those of the world cannot see or hear them.

There is no real physical barrier between that side and this. The other side has a clear vision of what is happening in the world while most men and women simply see the world reflected back at them; not seeing or hearing anything in that other plane or dimension.

The Gateway of the Cross is a portal, a two-way opening between the world and the place of angels and God. From that blessed vantage it is possible to stay in the world even while you have some awareness of what is happening beyond these earthly boundaries. The Gateway of the Cross is what allows us to remain in the world physically without being entirely a product of the world.

The Gateway is a spiritual place where we are able to communicate with God as well as continue to work in the world. The first challenge is finding the Gateway; the next is to properly manage the Gateway.

Making the Supernatural Simple

Being in the Gateway is being less than 100% in the presence of God while at the same time you are not totally in the physical world around you.

Have you heard of Skype? It is a way to video chat with someone in another place. It's like being on the phone but you can see who is on other end of the conversation as well as hear what is being said. Whatever the web camera picks up appears on your computer monitor.

(If you are technically gifted you may find some errors in my illustrations. I am not gifted with an understanding of these things and just do the best I can to get by. Please forgive any inadequacies on that front.)

You may be sitting in your home office in Georgia speaking to your sister in Oregon. You are able to see everything around you there in Georgia; your computer, your cat, the breeze blowing the sheers on your window, and hear the sound of the music your son is playing in his bedroom. While chatting with your sister you hear the honk of a car on the street outside and engine noise from your neighbor's lawn mower. You are obviously living in the daily reality of your Georgia home.

You are in Georgia using Skype while your sister sits at her kitchen table in Oregon. It may be 6 PM in your Georgia office but it is 3 PM in your sister's kitchen. Your reality is split because you are participating in two time zones simultaneously. Differences in time are only part of the story. Through the lens of the web cam on your sister's computer you can see her kitchen in Oregon, hear the bark of her dog in the background and see your niece frost cookies on the granite countertop.

You are not 100% in Georgia. Neither are you 100% in Oregon. Yet you can see, hear, and communicate in both places at once, as does your sister. If your nephew channel surfs on the family room television near your sister's kitchen while she is chatting with you, she is speaking in Georgia at the same time she is listening to be sure her son finally settles on an acceptable show. She is not 100% in Oregon or 100% in Georgia.

You may see, hear, and communicate in Georgia at the same time you are seeing, hearing, and communicating with Oregon. You are in

Oregon but not of Oregon. Your sister is in Georgia but not of Georgia.

This illustration is a hint of what the Spirit makes possible in the Gateway of the Cross. You see, hear, communicate, and participate in the world at the same time you see, hear, and communicate with the world beyond.

It might be easier for you to visualize the structure and purpose of the Gateway of the Cross if I explain what I mean by "Gateway."

Architecture of the Cross of Christ - Unlike Any Other

Every cross consists of two straight elements that meet somewhere along their length to form a fixed intersection. The Cross of Jesus Christ is unlike any other cross and has a continuing and present role in the life of every Christian.

The power of God comes to us through the vertical member of the cross. Our purpose as His children is to receive that power, become part of it, and then send it out again into the family and into the world. One way to understand the horizontal member of the cross is to think of it as a human conduit for Christ, a pathway for what is received from above to be shared with others in the world.

Spiritually speaking, the vertical member of the cross of Christ connects God and man. It doesn't matter what the actual dimension of the timbers were to which Christ was nailed. What is important is that the vertical tree was long enough to span the distance between heaven and earth. The Holy Spirit travels up and down this fantastic supernatural elevator as He goes about teaching those who are willing to learn.

The horizontal member of the cross of Christ is an earthly conduit that spans the divide between one child of God and another. The

[108]

point at which the vertical and horizontal members meet is the Gateway of the Cross. This is the spiritual portal that joins the world with what is beyond this world. The life and blessings of the Lord Jesus Christ flow down through the vertical member of the Cross so we may receive them. The part we play in the Gateway is one mechanism by which the truth and fact of Jesus Christ is shared with others in the world.

The will and Word of God become the power of the Holy Spirit. That same Spirit works through us when we allow it to pass through us via the outstretched member of the cross. Simply stated, God blesses us and we send that blessing out to others.

Every child of God will be burdened with the cares of the world and the needs of others. Some workers willingly take on the burdens of others as they are instructed by the Spirit. When the burdens of the world come into us they are dispersed into the hand of God by passing through us to ascend and rest at His feet after traveling through the vertical member of the Cross.

When you give something to Christ you let it go from your hand into the Gateway where earth and heaven meet. Like a hot ash rising up the chimney of a fireplace your burden floats up the vertical connection to God and the weight and care of it disappears. Giving away a sin, trouble, hurt, or problem to God only works if you have it properly packaged and send it off in the right place. That launching place is in the Gateway of the Cross where you are blessed with a direct connection to God made possible by the Holy Spirit.

A Heavenly Mansion on Earth

Jesus promises each child of the King a mansion in heaven, exclusively prepared and with no substitutions allowed. Not only is there a mansion waiting for you in the New Jerusalem but there is a mansion available to you today. The location of your present mansion is the Gateway of the Cross.

When you dream about heaven how do you imagine it will differ from your earthly walk? In heaven there will be no sadness, no pain, no loss, no failure, and no fear. Every moment will be peaceful, joyous, secure, filled with love, and there will be every provision made for you. Life in heaven is life lived in the fullness of relationship with God and in the presence of Jesus Christ.

All those heavenly things are available to you today in the Gateway. The lives of those who walk in every moment and circumstance with Jesus Christ live in peace, joy, provision, success, security, love, and without fear - even though the dust of world is visible on their boots. The Gateway is the place where heaven and earth meet. You will not experience the complete fullness of heaven in the Gateway but the Spirit does offer you a big down-payment on what is to come.

God provides a blessed dwelling for you on earth in the Gateway. Why would He not? His Spirit lives within you and a refuge is needed from the world. The Gateway of the Cross is a very safe place.

When God called you to Him through the Holy Spirit you were reborn as a new creation in Jesus Christ. The moment your human spirit combined with His a door to the Gateway opened for you. Not only are you able to be in the world without being of the world, but you may also accept the offer of heaven on earth. Have you done so?

"The Cross is the center of Time and Eternity, the answer to the enigmas of both.

The Cross is the exhibition of the nature of God, the gateway whereby any individual of the human race can enter into union with

God. When we get to the Cross, we do not go through it; we abide in the life to which the Cross is the gateway.

The Cross is the point where God and sinful man merge with a crash and the way to life is opened - but the crash is on the heart of God."
- Oswald Chambers, *My Utmost for His Highest*

Blocking the Gateway

Anytime you claim a right to yourself, to a private life apart from Christ, you create a spiritual blockage that makes it impossible for the power of the Cross to move through you. When you erect such a barrier to the work of the Spirit, any energy or blessing from God cannot travel into the world through you then out to the rest of the world as God intends. The Gateway of the Cross is closed by our unwillingness and the vertical aspect of the Cross that reaches up to heaven shuts down.

Think about the horizontal member of the Cross as a pipe. Then think of the choicest fruit God could possibly send descending from God's hand to yours through the Cross. That most delightful gift is meant to be shared. Even the most delectable fruit will eventually rot if caught in a pipe and emit a stench as its flesh decays. When God sends a blessing to you, whether magnificent or mean, it is to be shared. If you catch it tight in your hand and refuse to pass it on it will eventually spoil, blessing no one in the end.

Jesus said, *"Freely you have received, freely give."* - Matthew 10:8

If all you allow is a transmission of message, power, or spirit through the horizontal member you are completely in the world. The loop to the Spirit and the Lord is shut down. The Gateway to the Cross would be made moot if God allowed such a thing. He does not. If you insist on shutting that door He will slam another and you

[111]

will find yourself in the same predicament as Adam and Eve; evicted and the gate closed behind you. Unlike the original occupants of Eden, however, this gate can open once again to allow you partial entry. But re-entry requires you to give the Spirit free passage through you both upward and outward.

"So we are always confident, knowing that while we are at home in the body we are absent from the Lord. For we walk by faith, not by sight. We are confident, yes, well pleased rather to be absent from the body and to be present with the Lord." - 2 Corinthians 5:6-8

Proof that you live in the Gateway

The indwelling Spirit of Christ is evidence that you live in the Gateway. New creations see the sights of the world through new eyes; hear the sounds of the world through new ears; and speak with a voice changed from that which was before. The most compelling proof that you live with Christ in the Gateway is the way your view of temptation has changed. What once seemed a delectable morsel is now nothing but dust.

"If you are born again, the Spirit of God makes the alteration manifest in your actual life and reasoning, and when the crisis comes you are the most amazed person on earth at the wonderful difference there is in you." - Oswald Chambers, *My Utmost for His Highest*

[112]

False Teachers and Failed Leadership

"For the time has come for judgment to begin at the house of God; and if it begins with us first, what will be the end of those who do not obey the gospel of God?" - 1 Peter 4:17

Both scholars and Christians have studied, debated, argued, and prayed about the specifics of the Rapture for centuries. Such pursuits have two distinctly different purposes.

- Scholars seek to understand the data that exists in order to explain, to discuss, and to **study the concept** of Rapture.

- Christians study and pray in order to **participate** in the Rapture.

The Rapture is the first wave of the elect to make entrance into heaven. However, unless one is fit to spend eternity in the presence of God the details of the Rapture are meaningless. Scholarship without a relationship to Jesus Christ is the equivalent of spinning wheels that go nowhere.

What does the Bible teach about the criteria for entrance into heaven? The requirements for Rapture are spelled out in scripture. Since it is possible to know what it takes to be fit for heaven, betting your life on Rapture Roulette is fool's work. It is only possible to be fit for Rapture by the grace of God and the power of the Holy Spirit. Jesus Christ paid the full price to redeem you. That price was His shed blood.

The Holy Spirit makes it possible for fallen men and women to become new creations through Christ Jesus. [2 Corinthians 5:17] The power of the Spirit allows you to remain balanced in the Gateway and keeps you ready to fly when called to meet Jesus in the air.

Do not be deceived by pretty words from the pulpit

There is a growing incidence of false teaching that parades as the Gospel in many pulpits across the world. A major theme in the last half of the New Testament is the caution against false prophets and wrong teaching.

Much, if not most, of the preaching on Sunday morning is based on false prophecy. This is the End Time and the Bible warns against this sign of the last days. Don't be surprised. God told us this would happen.

"A wonderful and horrible thing is committed in the land. The prophets prophesy falsely, and the priests bear rule by their means; and my people love to have it so: and what will ye do in the end thereof?" -- Jeremiah 5:30-31

Is asking Jesus into your heart a requirement for Rapture? Some of the largest denominations in the United States teach that even this small act is unnecessary. In 2009 the Evangelical Lutheran Church in America (ELCA) adopted a policy of "whatever works for you is okay by us."

"What else is this, than either to make God a liar, or to doubt His truth -- that is, to attribute truth to ourselves, but to God falsehood and levity? In doing this, is not man denying God and setting himself up as an idol in his own heart?" - Martin Luther, *Concerning Christian Liberty*

The ELCA today operates in stark contrast to the precepts of its namesake and author of its original doctrine. Practicing homosexuals may serve in church leadership and in the pulpit. Abortion rights are approved by this same "if it feels good do it" doctrine. Presiding ELCA Bishop Hanson said he did not understand why the issue of homosexuality gets everybody so worked up since Jesus Himself never mentioned the subject.

Don't Be Fooled by Red-Letter Rationalization

Many Bibles print the words of Jesus in red letters. Some preachers believe that the only verses in the Bible with any authority are those printed in red and that if Jesus didn't say it then it doesn't count.

God is a fact. Anything God says is important. The Bible is the Word of God. Jesus is the Word. Jesus is God. Jesus is the Holy Spirit. The Holy Spirit is God. Every word in the Bible may as well be printed in red letters. Either all of it is relevant or none of it is.

Any statement from God in the Old Testament is a statement from Christ. There are many who suggest that the standard for Christian behavior is what is printed in red letters and you have their permission to forget the rest. If you exclude the parts of the Bible that are not the words of Jesus you exclude everything that proceeds from the Father and the Holy Spirit.

The deity professed by the ELCA is merely god. This symbolic god has been smoothed, shaped, and molded to fit the desires of the people who make the rules. The ELCA has made the choice between God and Not God. Not God won. If their god was God they would know that the only rules that matter are God's rules.

Since much of the Bible has been rendered meaningless and any opinion about the intent and meaning of Jesus' words is as good as any other, why do denominations like the ELCA even pretend to care about Christ born, Christ crucified, Christ resurrected, and Christ about to return?

The sad truth is they don't care. They speak and pray to jesus born, jesus crucified, jesus resurrected, and some jesus who will come again. The problem is there is no real jesus. There was no real birth, no horrible crucifixion, no glorious resurrection, and there will be no return of this jesus who never was.

So, is it true that all you need do to be saved and rapture-ready is to ask Jesus into your heart? The answer is 'Yes' if the savior who responds is Jesus Christ of the Bible and is the very Person who perished on the Cross for you. No human may change, interpret, or limit this Christ. He is, He always has been, and He always will be.

But the question is not as simple as you may have been led to believe. To ask Jesus into your heart as your personal Savior means you must clear your heart of any other allegiance, any other idol, and any doctrine other than what is found in the Word of God as revealed by the Holy Spirit. In order to be a new creation in Christ you must actually *change*. There is no other option.

In a 2005 interview, Larry King asked a prominent mega-church minister to share his opinions about abortion and same-sex marriages. The minister replied, "You know what, Larry? I don't go there." Mr. King then inquired if the mega-church minister ever used the word "sinners," he said, "I don't use it. I never thought about it. But I probably don't."

There was a huge uproar within the minister's church following this interview, but not about his refusal to take a position on abortion or the practice of homosexuality. The outcry was about a far more fundamental question of Christian faith. The mega-church icon was unable, even after Larry King gave him numerous opportunities, to clarify his position on the path to eternal life. The minister would not state that Jesus was the only way, *since there were many good people with pagan beliefs, so he just couldn't really say…*

[116]

The attempt by church leadership to side-step *any* issue should set off warning alarms. Christ is a solid foundation, not some plastic boat in a kiddie pool that floats here and drifts there, changing course with each puff of breeze.

Easy is Useless, Leadership is Bold

What good is a spiritual leader who really doesn't want to talk about the most difficult, confusing, seamy, and nastiest questions of human life as they relate to our walk with God? Folks in this messed up world don't need to hear feel-good preaching, they need to hear that there is a life and death choice to be made and it must be made now.

"Let's all just get along. Each to their own and let's go have a cup of coffee and a doughnut."

That sums up the doctrinal positions of many preachers today. They elevate fellowship over righteousness. If it is more important for you to stay in the good graces of your buddies than to be in right relationship with Jesus Christ then you'll be in good company when the church is called to Glory and you all are left behind --together.

It's easy to talk about love and goodwill. It's easy to condemn what everyone else condemns and rejoice in what everyone else rejoices in. *Easy* will not cut it any longer and there is only one source that establishes what may be rightly condemned and what is a true cause of rejoicing. That one source is God's Word, given to you in the Bible and in the person of Jesus Christ. The Holy Spirit makes it possible for you to be joined now and forever in union with God the Father and Christ the Son.

I don't know if there was ever a time when easy worked. It certainly won't in this End Time.

"Do you not know that the unrighteous will not inherit the kingdom of God? Do not be deceived. Neither fornicators, nor idolaters, nor adulterers, nor homosexuals, nor sodomites, nor thieves, nor covetous, nor drunkards, nor revilers, nor extortioners will inherit the kingdom of God. And such were some of you. But you were washed, but you were sanctified, but you were justified in the name of the Lord Jesus and by the Spirit of our God."
- 1 Corinthians 6:11

The only way you may stand before a Holy God is to arrive sinless. The only possible way to become sinless is through the finished work of Jesus Christ on the Cross.

Imagine you prayed the Sinner's Prayer a month ago and the preacher announced that, "You are saved!" In the past month did you lie? Have sex with anyone to whom you are not married? Closed a slick business deal that barely fell on the legal side of fraud?

Any of these behaviors could exclude you from the kingdom of God. These are doubtless some bad, bad behaviors, but what does God think about more mundane behaviors in the twenty-first century among enlightened folk?

Are you a fan of rap music? Which comedians do you listen to? What video games do you play? What television programs do you watch? How do you speak to your friends, your teachers, your family members?

What exactly do the terms *filthiness*, *foolish talking*, and *coarse jesting* mean to you? You don't need to define them for me; you need to define them for yourself. My opinion doesn't matter. God will judge how closely your definitions match His because any of these errors will disqualify you from entrance to heaven. [Ephesians 5:3-6]

[118]

Entrance to the kingdom of God is impossible for mortal men, but through the Holy Spirit all things become possible. Jesus Christ alone holds the key to the Narrow Gate.

The Rise and Fall of the Church Age

"I know your works that have a name that you are alive, but you are dead." - Revelation 3:1

The period between the Ascension of Jesus and the day of the Rapture is commonly referred to as the Church Age. The church of Christ has had its problems since the day after Jesus returned to heaven. How can we know that we will not be left behind since none of us will be completely sinless while we still draw breath on this earth?

What is the name some have that is supposed to indicate life? That name is Christian. Yet, most who identify themselves with that name are not alive with the Holy Spirit but dead in the world. The message to the church of Sardis [Revelation 3:1] equally applies to those in the waning church age. Most folks who accept the Christian label are not alive in Christ, but just as dead spiritually as some of the congregants in Sardis. Only the ready and waiting are free of worry. The Lord says He will come as a thief and those who aren't ready, those without the new life with the Holy Spirit, will be left behind.

It's a difficult time be a scriptural Christian in the world today. (By "scriptural Christian" I mean those who believe the Bible is the inerrant and infallible Word of God.) Jesus knows our circumstances. Nothing that is happening in our nation or in the world is either a surprise to Him or unexpected. If you have been faithful to study God's Word with the guidance of the Holy Spirit you shouldn't be surprised either.

Jesus knows your works. He has opened a door to heaven that no one can shut. What we are asked to do in this time is to keep the Word in our heart and Christ's name on our lips. [Revelation 3:8] What is the promise Jesus makes to those who profess faith without reserve and who persevere in the trials of our day?

"Because you have kept My command to persevere, I also will keep you from the hour of trial which shall come upon the whole world, to test those who dwell on the earth." - Revelation 3:10

Those who are left behind in the Rapture aren't necessarily doomed but they will be sorely tested by the events of the tribulation.

How would you describe your present circumstances? Is your faith strong and vibrant or are you simply *hoping* that you will hear the Call? Is the name of Jesus Christ on your tongue or have you put a relationship with Him on hold until a more convenient time? Are you waiting for God to work a miracle before you make that final commitment?

Are you fooling yourself about being a Christian? Read Revelation 3:9 again and use the word *Christian* instead of Jew. Invite the Holy Spirit into each crevice of your spirit and every secret place of your heart and mind. Once He enters the cleansing process begins. The process is bound to get messy, but as long as your spiritual remodeling and repair is underway the chains that bind you to this world are broken.

Passing from Darkness into Light

The church age began when the soft loving glow of Christ's sacrifice on Calvary illuminated the eastern foothills on Resurrection morning. Once Jesus returned to His Father the Light went out from the world and darkness began to slowly spread from east to west and north to south. [1 John 2:8]

The Light of the World was welcomed into Jerusalem with palm branches and a parade accompanied by shouts of Hosanna! [John 12:13] For a few days Jesus taught all who first welcomed Him before He was betrayed, arrested, mocked, abused and beaten to the point where He was no longer recognizable. And then He was crucified.

As Christ struggled through His final moments on the Cross the sun failed and darkness descended upon the world. The Light was gone. [Luke 23:44-46]

The Bible is like a knitted sweater; if you pull one piece of yarn the whole string eventually follows with no break or separation from beginning to end. God speaks of particular concepts or truths many times throughout His Word.

The intricacy and inter-weavings of the Bible proves it to be a God-breathed message. Nearly every verse has multiple meanings and it grows and morphs as the Spirit dictates to every soul who studies it by faith. The words and stories of the Bible are true in not only the literal sense, but apply to the present time of every generation as well as to future events. Each message on a page of the Bible is also somehow related to every other message regardless of its location between Genesis 1 and Revelation 22. The order of events during Jesus' last days as a mortal have been repeated in the course of the church age as well as in the life of every man, woman, and child who initiates a relationship with the Lord.

In the beginning we all shouted Hosanna when we enthusiastically entered into relationship with the Holy Spirit. And one day, every

[123]

person who accepted Jesus as Lord will deny him. Each one of us will fail Him.

At that point one of two things will happen. Some will die to and with Christ, only to rise again to continue their walk in faith. And some will go the way of Judas, selling out to the world and leaving the relationship that once began with such joy and promise. Those who choose Christ will remain in the light of love that emanates from the face of God.

Judas remained with the world and died alone in it, consumed by flames until the embers and ashes cooled and all became as dark as eternal night.

Do you walk in the light? *If we say that we have fellowship with Him, and walk in darkness, we lie and do not practice the truth.* [1 John 1:5-6.] In God there is no darkness, only light. If we believe we follow the path of right relationship with Jesus Christ we cannot walk in darkness. There is no darkness in the vicinity of our Lord.

The Angel of Light, our enemy, is crafty and offers a source of illumination intended to confuse us and draw us away from the true source of salvation. The light of Jesus Christ is soft and will not burn anyone in His presence. It is a comforting light that never dims and is a constant source of direction and security.

Worldly eyes are drawn to the light from the Enemy; vivid, intense, and passionate. There is only one outcome for a candle that burns on both ends - darkness that comes twice as fast as a candle lit on only one end. The passions of the world lead to death by fire. The light of the Enemy is the furnace of Daniel and will incinerate all who stand near it. The world is a burning barn. Moses watched in amazement, fear, and awe as God spoke from a bush that burned but was not consumed in the flames. The family of Jesus Christ will witness and experience the fire as it first smolders and then spreads.

Like the Burning Bush, we will not be consumed by the flame. And, when that refining fire has accomplished its purpose the door of the blazing furnace will open and the hand of Jesus Christ himself will draw us into his full resurrected presence.

Revelation

The two messages of **Rapture and Revelation** are (1) this is the End Time and (2) a choice is required of you. No other book in the Bible is so studiously avoided or more difficult to understand than John's Revelation of Jesus Christ. Few pastors take on the symbolism and relevance of the book of Revelation in their normal sermon rotation.

Highly regarded scholars and pastors disagree on what the book of Revelation means. God is appointing messengers throughout the world to ask the family of Jesus Christ to listen for His voice. The Shepherd is calling His flock to return to the fold. Messengers called to evangelize seek those predestined for eternal life but who are not yet united with the flock.

This is the End Time and you must choose God (Jesus Christ) or Not God. The purpose of this book is to challenge you to know *why* you believe what you believe. Many people believe they are Rapture-ready when in fact Jesus doesn't recognize them as family members. There are absolutes and there are conditions to relationship with Christ. The book of Revelation addresses the subject of the End Time and what a right relationship with Jesus looks like.

"The time is near for those things which must shortly take place." [Revelation 1:1-3]

The ministry that began with simple fishermen in the first century rapidly expanded to include others in a wide variety of life circumstances - and today that model is being repeated. The seven churches of Revelation to whom Jesus addressed the letters of Chapters 2, 3, and 4 were actual churches in John's time. These seven churches also represent the progression of the church age from its beginning in the first century until now.

These seven letters also describe Christians and congregations today. Only the supernatural Word of God could create seven letters that were relevant at the time they were written, represent the seven progressive eras of the church age historically, and also represent present day churches.

Have your Bible handy for this next section. It includes many references to verses in Revelation.

The Church at Ephesus

The condition of the church at Ephesus is similar to many of the "faithful" today.

"I know your works, your labor, your patience, and that you cannot bear those who are evil. And you have tested those who say they are apostles and are not, and have found them liars; and you have persevered and have patience, and have labored for My name's sake and have not become weary. Nevertheless I have this against you, that you have left your first love. Remember therefore from where you have fallen; repent and do the first works, or else I will come to you quickly and remove your lampstand from its place—unless you repent." - Revelation 2:2-5

Jesus tells Ephesus that His standards are high, very high. The Ephesian church wasn't populated by novices, but rather by veterans of the battle of being in the world but not of the world. What love. What passion. What hope. What dedication. What commitment.

After twenty years of marriage it can be difficult to stir up the embers of passion to honeymoon levels. New love daydreams about its beloved and wonders what gift or service it can offer. New love never argues over money, kids, the remote control, or who forgot to feed the dog. First love tends to disappear when real life moves in to stay.

Do you remember how you looked at your bride (or groom) just before you took your marriage vows? Jesus Christ requires our first love every day of every year. The letter to the church of Ephesus in Revelation speaks directly to those of us who surrendered to real life. Now is the time to remember just how devoted we are to Jesus Christ and return to our first passionate and abiding love for our Savior.

The Church at Smyrna

The saints of Smyrna were similar to obedient children of God throughout the church age. In this letter Christ recognizes the faithfulness and hardship suffered by church members. People who masquerade as Christians speak evil against them calling evil good, and good, evil. [Revelation 2:9] Christian groups condemn one another based on different views on alcohol, divorce, politics, education, evolution, homosexuality, and abortion. Jesus' letter to Smyrna reveals that absolute truth absolutely exists. Only one side of such debate over good and evil is absolutely right -- the side of Jesus Christ.

There is a church of Smyrna today. Membership belongs to those who believe that the Bible is the inerrant Word of God, that Jesus is who the Bible says He is, and that He holds us to a standard that is not negotiable. The present day church of Smyrna loves Jesus, follows His commands, and will, if necessary, be obedient unto death.

Jesus was well aware of the worldly poverty and suffering of the church at Smyrna, yet he called them "rich." And indeed, there is no earthly measure for the peace, joy, and security that life in the Gateway offers through relationship with Christ.

The congregation at Smyrna lived in a wicked community, "where Satan dwells." [Revelation 2:13] The world has become a wicked place in the 21st century and Satan is the present ruler of the world today just as he was in Smyrna.

"Do not fear any of those things which you are about to suffer. ... Be faithful unto death, and I will give you the crown of life." - Revelation 2:10

This verse doesn't mean we will all be thrown into prison or in any way conveys the manner of our deaths; it says most simply, *Do not become weary, but persevere and be patient.* Then, like the church at Smyrna, Christ will have nothing to hold against us and eternity in His presence is assured. [Revelation 2:11] The Smyrna church was ready for Rapture.

The Church at Pergamos

The folks in Pergamos seem to have been a very tolerant bunch. Still, the members worshipped Jesus Christ as Lord and Savior even when the road became difficult.

But the membership tolerated communion with idolaters. This church taught relativism to their children and preached conditional righteousness. Holiness allows no compromise, no "buts", and no exceptions. There also seemed to be an issue of sexual immorality - in thought, word, deed, attire, and entertainment. How many churches today fit the same description as Pergamos? [Revelation 2:14-16]

Jesus requires repentance from such error and sin just as He did in the first century. Jesus has not changed. Those who overcome are

[130]

promised food and strength in the bread of Heaven and the acquittal from sin. [Revelation 2:17]

The Church at Thyatira

In this letter Jesus identifies Himself as the Son of God with eyes like a flame of fire. Jesus Christ addresses Thyatira in the role of judge and not as Shepherd.

The beginning of the letter is a glowing recitation of the great works of the church at Thyatira. This was a congregation who performed great service working for others. On paper this group looked great and was doing more and more rather than less and less.

"I know your works, love, service, faith, and your patience; and as for your works, the last are more than the first." - Revelation 2:19

Simply being busy working for the Lord is not enough. Churches today with the greatest outreach programs, service to community and the poor, or with the most extensive evangelical ministries will not be acceptable to Christ on the basis of those works alone. Thyatira was a church of great works - and great immorality. Jesus promised the morning star to those who did not tolerate the behavior of their errant brethren. The rest would be left to their depravity and tribulation.

What 'prophet' or 'prophetess' seduces church members today with teachings that abortion or the practice of homosexuality is acceptable? Which televangelists would argue that it's okay to use what is given to God to support their own extravagant lifestyles?

Those who belong to present day churches like Thyatira have the opportunity to separate and hold fast to what they have until Christ returns. That opportunity comes with an expiration date.

[131]

The Church at Sardis

The church at Sardis appears to have been on spiritual life support. The Sardis church was made up of christians who worshipped god and jesus. They used the right terminology but their religion was one of symbolism and not the absolute truth of Christ. [Revelation 3:1] Yet even within this dead church there were still a few who knew the real Christ.

Why do you belong to your church? Do the leaders and members speak the right words but produce no living works? Are you among the few names [Revelation 3:4] in your church who eagerly await the call to join Christ?

"Be watchful, and strengthen the things which remain, that are ready to die" - Revelation 3:2

Stand on the truth of Jesus Christ and not religious doctrine. Religions are about to die. The only way to overcome is by a personal relationship with Christ. There is no proxy and there is no excuse. [Revelation 3:5]

The Church at Philadelphia

Like the church at Smyrna, Christ found nothing to hold against the folks in Philadelphia. Christ opened the door to eternal relationship with the Philadelphians which no one could shut because they were faithful in their works, in obedience to God's Word, and professing one Name above all others. [Revelation 3:8]

Another characteristic the Philadelphia church had in common with Smyrna was persecution at the hand of established "Christians" who claimed the label but not the One to whom the label refers. Note the similarities between Revelation 2:9 and 3:9.

[132]

You will find this same prophetic message in John 16:2: "They will put you out of the synagogue; in fact, the time is coming when anyone who kills you will think they are offering a service to God." The blessed news is that Jesus has overcome those who persecute His faithful [John 16:33] and makes a promise above all promises for those of us in this End Time:

*"Because you have kept My command to persevere, **I also will keep you from the hour of trial** which shall come upon the whole world, to test those who dwell on the earth."* - Revelation 3:10

The hour of trial in verse 10 refers to the Tribulation and is a significant biblical reference used to support the belief in pretribulation Rapture. Noted prophetic scholar Dr. John Walvoord shares this view in his 1966 book, *The Revelation of Jesus Christ*, pg. 87:

"Many have understood that the preposition "from" (Greek ek) is best understood as "out of" rather than simply "from." ... If this promise has any bearing on the question of pretribulationism, however, what is said emphasizes deliverance from rather than deliverance through."

In other words, the perseverance of the Philadelphia church received a promise of escape from the Tribulation and not simply an assurance of strength to endure the trials soon to come.

Christians in this End Time face their own hour of trial, of testing. Why do you believe what you believe? Have you truly made a choice for God rather than Not God? Are you a Christian or a christian? The test is being administered and proctored by the Holy Spirit. No one may answer for you and there are no make-up exams.

The Church at Laodicea

What is the greatest danger to modern Christians? I suggest it is the ease of our lives, the absence of real *need* and the enjoyment of all available comforts that don't seem to require faith. Without a need why seek a savior?

"I know your works, that you are neither cold nor hot. I could wish you were cold or hot. So then, because you are lukewarm, and neither cold nor hot, I will vomit you out of My mouth. Because you say, 'I am rich, have become wealthy, and have need of nothing'— and do not know that you are wretched, miserable, poor, blind, and naked—" - Revelation 3:15-17

We are wealthy, comfortable, and the little we have learned from scientific advancements throughout the past 150 years has made us errantly confident in our position, possessions, professions, and self-confidence.

The last church to receive a letter was Laodicea. The state of that church describes the state of many in the body of Christ today - lukewarm and self-important. There is no true wealth apart from Christ and no earthly garment will clothe us once we leave the world.

Jesus rebuked the Laodiceans for their ignorance and self-satisfaction. Have you felt the Holy Spirit whispering that you have not yet perfected your walk? Have you been even the tiniest bit unsettled with your routine? Jesus is nothing if not faithful and by his "rebuke and chastening" you may be positive that He loves you. [Revelation 3:19]

Jesus Christ stands at the door of our churches, our capitols, our schools, our homes, and our hearts. Only those who hear His voice will open the door that He may enter. [Revelation 3:20]

Most churches today preach relative morality, steering away from messages of absolute truth that seem *intolerant*. There are many Laodiceans in the world today who esteem the goodwill of their fellow men more than the goodwill of Jesus Christ. The distraction of such error drowns out the sound of Christ's knock on the door. And so He turns away.

Jesus Christ is no longer welcome in public schools, in the great legislative halls of our nation or in most other public places. Laodiceans don't ruffle feathers, they simply try to get along believing they are being open-minded and playing by the rules. Christians seek to share the mind of Christ, not to be open minded. Christ asks us to repent of our politically correct behavior and to make an undiluted, unconditional commitment to Him.

Have you worked diligently for earthly comforts? How does your passion for the material quality-of-life measures compare to your love for Jesus? Are you truly passionate about Jesus or just kind of lukewarm? You must choose today if you will serve the world or the Shepherd. [Joshua 24:15]

The Shepherd Calls - Will You Respond?

The earthquake in Japan was a far louder call than the soft knocking of Jesus on any closed door or heart. Continuing disasters and tumult across the globe combine to amplify His voice. Yet, in each of them there is a still small voice.

God is providing obvious and cumulative evidence of the Savior's call. *Rapture and Revelation* is an additional method of delivery for the same message. Across Christendom the voice of the Shepherd is calling. Do you hear? Will you respond?

"He who has an ear, let him hear what the Spirit says to the churches." - Revelation 3:22

The Promise

The door to heaven has been opened and the Lord is beginning to fulfill the prophecy of the End Time. We are there.

"After these things I looked, and behold, a door standing open in heaven. And the first voice which I heard was like a trumpet speaking with me, saying, "Come up here, and I will show you things which must take place after this." - Revelation 4:1

What is the message John shares with us in verse one? The door to heaven is open. When Christ died on the cross He shattered the barrier between this world and the next, leaving the door open so His sheep may pass between its narrow gateposts.

"Come up here." John doesn't say that God, or any of His servants, snatched him into the Spirit. The trumpeting voice said, "Come." John was willing. John was obedient. John arrived.

Rejoice - Be Comforted

"...and behold, a throne set in heaven, and One sat on the throne. And He who sat there was like a jasper and a sardius stone in appearance; and there was a rainbow around the throne, in appearance like an emerald." - Revelation 4:2-3

God is still on His throne, gloriously resplendent in precious gems and fully in control. There is nothing to worry about with Jesus Christ as Savior and Lord. [Psalm 27:1] His work is sufficient and complete. The door to heaven is now open and Jesus has begun the final battle of the war.

Heaven's door is described as a narrow gate through which few will enter. [Matthew 7:13-14] The door is open and beckons us, "Come."

Will you?

The Eve of Rapture

"And it will be when you say, 'Why does the LORD our God do all these things to us?' then you shall answer them, 'Just as you have forsaken Me and served foreign gods in your land, so you shall serve aliens in a land that is not yours.'" - Jeremiah 5:19

Those who are left behind after the Rapture of the Church will either serve the god of the world or pay the price for refusing to bow to Satan. This world is not the home of the family of Jesus Christ.

The State of the Nuclear Family

There is no doubt that the call of the Shepherd's voice is being carried from one end of the earth to the other on the winds of the Holy Spirit. Time is running out and the choice between God and Not God must be made today. To choose God is to accept the truth of Jesus Christ. Any other option is the choice of Not God.

The members of the family of Jesus Christ are getting closer to one another and strengthening their bonds. Many nuclear families are also experiencing changes in the way they interact with each other. One of three things will happen to your own family as you journey through this End Time.

1. Families will be reunited.

Have you experienced a change in your own family dynamic? I pray you have and that the change knits each one closer to the other. Families who were scattered to the four winds like the seeds of a mature dandelion head are finding their way back to foundational family relationships and homesteads.

[139]

There is an increasing number of successful people returning to their home towns after years of living elsewhere. Brothers and sisters are bringing their children back to the place where they grew up. Grandparents and grandchildren, nieces and nephews, and cousins galore are finally building their own bonds of family.

2. Family ties will be strained to the breaking point.

Other families are finding that the gaps between members are getting even wider. The ties that bind family members together are losing their elasticity. Telephone calls have changed to emails or text messages. Conversations about truly important concepts, events, and issues are passionless, shallower, and the petals of the family flower are beginning to turn brown at the edges.

"So He said to them, 'Assuredly, I say to you, there is no one who has left house or parents or brothers or wife or children, for the sake of the kingdom of God, who shall not receive many times more in this present time, and in the age to come eternal life.'" -
Luke 18:29-30

3. Families will maintain the Status Quo.

In other families there is no noticeable change at all. Everything continues on an even keel because the family is already living with a *shared faith* in Christ or a shared *absence of faith* in Christ.

Christians are not only separated from people, groups, and practices that behave or accept things we cannot, but being separated unto Christ can also create very real practical difficulties within a family unit.

"Now the LORD had said to Abram:

'Get out of your country,
From your family
And from your father's house,
To a land that I will show you.'" - Genesis 12:1

"By faith Abraham obeyed when he was called to go out to the place which he would receive as an inheritance. And he went out, not knowing where he was going." - Hebrews 11:8

Is it any wonder that our earthly families are experiencing the same strains and pressures that the Church is? How could they not? Ever since Adam was gifted with Eve the family unit has been the heart of man's walk of earth, and is the basis for relationship that defines the Father and Son in the Trinity.

Indeed, the first odor of the End Time began drifting on the breeze of history when the family began to decay. Fast forward to today. Look at the stark contrast between what a family used to be in decades and centuries past compared to the definition of a family today.

The term *family* used to refer to people related to one another by marriage, adoption, or birth. *Alternative lifestyle arrangements* now qualify for family status. A single person living alone is now considered a family. Cohabitating couples of any sexual combination (man and woman, man and man, or woman and woman) may also be considered a family. The increased acceptance and change in state laws of such alternative lifestyle arrangements have pretty much reduced the definition of family to "whatever."

The unwillingness to limit the definition of family has also affected the family of Jesus Christ. False teachers will tell you that love is all that matters. "Jesus came to save all." And, "everyone is in the family of Jesus Christ whether they know Him or not." There is an

[141]

absolute definition of who is in the family of Christ and who is not. God established the definition and it has not changed since Genesis.

The Timeline of Humanity is Nearing Its End

The timeline of human history is nearing its end. There will be no more signs at this juncture. We have arrived at the actual beginning of judgment. My hope is that the church of Jesus Christ will indeed be raptured at the beginning of Revelation chapter 4 (as most pretribulationists believe) and will not return to earth until the Bride of Christ appears arrayed in splendor in Revelation chapter 19. This is the time to unstop your ears and listen for the still small voice that is calling you to the fold. The call is not necessarily one of geography, but a call to return to your first love, to repent, to abstain from immorality, to associate with the brethren and separate yourself spiritually from Jezebel and her kind.

We are in the eleventh hour and the vineyard owner is making his last offer for workers to enter his vineyard. [Matthew 20:1-16] The practical message from this parable is the warning it brings to those who have been riding the fence. The reward for work in the vineyard was the same regardless of when the works began; but note that no man was offered employment more than once.

The Holy Spirit is offering employment in the form of relationship with Jesus Christ. There will not be another opportunity to accept employment if this one is refused.

The Measure of Faith

How do you know if you have been swayed by false teaching? Is your faith real or the product of unfounded hope? Are you certain you believe what you do based on God's Word and not the words of men? There is only one practical measurement with any ability to accurately reflect faith in Jesus Christ. This is a measurement or test you may only perform on yourself to determine your level of faith. You cannot apply it to someone else.

That measurement is fear. Just as a finite space cannot be occupied by two forms of matter at the same time, faith and fear cannot occupy any part of our spirit simultaneously. When faith moves in fear moves out, and vice versa. If you harbor any fear at all your faith is not yet perfected.

Fear is washed away when the fire hose of the cleansing Spirit increases our faith. Faith and a peace that passes all understanding are linked together by an unbreakable bond. The proof of faith is the degree of peace in our heart. [Hebrews 11:1]

There Were Only Eight

How many will actually meet Jesus in the air in the Rapture? What is the number of the remnant of Israel? How many Gentiles are truly adopted sons of God, ready to greet the Bridegroom when He comes?

The first clue of how tiny the number may be is found in the Genesis account of the flood. The humans of the world practiced evil, yet they still had families, loved their newborn babies, and there were many small children running about.

Do you remember how many people God sealed into the Ark? Eight. Paul (quoting Isaiah) reminds us [Romans 9:27-29] that even though the children of Israel were once numbered as the sands of the sea only a small remnant would be saved. If God saved eight the first time He destroyed the world, why would you think there will be masses lifted out the next time? It has never been His habit to save all, just the chosen and just the righteous.

[143]

When Elijah wailed before the Lord [1 Kings 19:14] that he was the last prophet God told him that 7,000 others had also been reserved for His purpose. No matter how alone we feel in this Sodom-like world today there are many more that we have yet to meet. Elijah was not the last, nor are we. But Elijah was one of a very few, and so may we also be.

Those in the secular world protest vehemently that God would not be so cruel as to require adherence to His word and relationship with His Son in order to enter heaven. Paul tells such protestors that only the elect have obtained such status with God and the rest have been given spirits of stupor, eyes that do not see and ears that do not hear. [Romans 11:7-8]

If the church is raptured on a Sunday morning do you imagine that there might be entire Christian congregations left intact? I believe there might be many. Entire denominations preach a spirit of stupor to their congregants. Eyes have glazed over and ears are so out of tune that the lies sound plausible. *Don't worry, be happy.*

False doctrines, false teaching, false preaching, and those who buy into the falsehoods without bothering to check every concept against the Word of God will not be raptured. Salvation is not for all. Not all nice people will be saved.

The only path to salvation was established before the heavens ever separated from the earth. Folks who believe the falsehoods being spread by their pastors will go home after church Rapture morning to the news that something strange happened in the world. Their church was unaffected - at least for the moment.

These churches preach a different gospel; they preach a jesus who is an antichrist. What is the difference between a christian church that preaches the gospel of jesus christ and a Christian church that

[144]

preaches the Gospel of Jesus Christ? The difference is life and death. Ask the church at Sardis.

Saints in the End Time

What will your experience be in the End Time? As mainstream denominations continue to devolve from Christianity to christianity, those with eyes to see and ears to hear will be evicted from the congregation. Some christians have already decided to remain in congregations with false preachers knowing full well that Jesus is no longer welcome.

Many in the body of Christ have already separated from their home congregations. Relationship with the very real person of Jesus Christ set them apart from their brothers and sisters who pray to another jesus. Some were accused of being unloving, extreme, dangerous, fanatical, intolerant, or even evil. Faith and devotion to the true Jesus Christ is blasphemy to the doctrine of false teachers and those who line up behind them.

"Christianity begins where religion ends...with the resurrection." – Herbert Booth Smith

Religion draws people to communion with the world. Relationship with Jesus Christ may require you to walk away from friends and family in order to remain in the presence of the Lord.

Tearing away from what is familiar will be difficult at first. Living in a world of creeping darkness and evil, and knowing that many you love have chosen to remain in the world is heart-breaking.

Where there is bad news there is also good news. One of the most remarkable things about the Bible is how each part applies to the time it was written, to history past, and also to a time yet to be. The ninth chapter of Ezekiel speaks to the prophet's time, to the first

Passover that broke Pharaoh's resolve to stop the exodus, and yet also applies to us in this present time.

Choose while you still can

Ezekiel 9 addresses the choice you must make between God or Not God. There will be a specific moment when that choice is removed from the table and any opportunity for relationship with Jesus Christ will no longer be possible. God is a precise God. He is a jealous God. He is a Holy God. God acts in real ways in actual places on real people.

Moses was specific in his instructions to the Israelites as they prepared for Passover. Blood from the sacrificed lamb was smeared on their doorposts as a mark of faithfulness lest the firstborn die. No blood, no exemption. No blood, death comes to the house. God made preparations for His faithful to be marked when the angels carried death through Egypt.

Ezekiel tells about another mark provided by God to save His people.

"Have you seen this, O son of man? Is it a trivial thing to the house of Judah to commit the abominations which they commit here? For they have filled the land with violence; then they have returned to provoke Me to anger." - Ezekiel 8:17

"And the LORD said to him, 'Go through the midst of the city, through the midst of Jerusalem, and put a mark on the foreheads of the men who sigh and cry over all the abominations that are done within it.'" - Ezekiel 9:4

God condemned to an immediate death all who did not wear His mark. Like the blood on the doorposts of the first Passover, God was specific about who would live and who would die. Praise God if you sigh and cry over all the abominations in the world today. Your weeping means you are God's own and will be spared the Tribulation to come.

The bad news is that God does not change. He is still precise. There is no lamb's blood for this time; there is no actual mark in this time; but there is still a specific requirement if you want to be passed over from certain death. That requirement begins and ends with Jesus Christ. No god, jesus, or spirit can save you. Pursue relationship with Jesus Christ. Check all you believe against the truth of God's Word.

"Most assuredly, I say to you that you will weep and lament, but the world will rejoice; and you will be sorrowful, but your sorrow will be turned into joy." - John 16:20

The realities of both the End Time and eternity-to-be are clear. In this world Christians will have tribulation, but we have reason for hope, for cheer, and for a fearless faith because Jesus has overcome the world. [John 16:33] It is time to make your final choice. There is no more time on the clock.

The End of Your Story

"For I testify to everyone who hears the words of the prophecy of this book: If anyone adds to these things, God will add to him the plagues that are written in this book; and if anyone takes away from the words of the book of this prophecy, God shall take away his part from the Book of Life, from the holy city, and from the things which are written in this book." - Revelation 22:18-19

There is only one source of Truth. Nothing may be rightly added or taken away from the truth of God's Word. It really does matter *why* you believe *what* you believe. There is only one Way to heaven and eternal life. The church of Jesus Christ will be raptured. There will be tribulation saints but I don't want to be one, do you?

It would be easy to be overwhelmed by the requirements of being Rapture-ready. Can anyone really be that righteous and still be human? The Apostle Paul lived an exemplary life of witness, service, and perseverance to the early church and every Christian since. Yet even he admitted his simple humanity in this verse; *"For what I am doing, I do not understand. For what I will to do, that I do not practice; but what I hate, that I do"*. - Romans 7:15

As long as you are willing, God will be sure you are able to both hear and respond when the Shepherd calls you home. New creations in Christ aren't 30-day wonders or one act plays. We are flesh and blood people on a journey of continuing discovery, transformation, and purpose to become more like Jesus every day by the Grace of God.

The end of your story was written two millennia ago and there will be no rewrite. Jesus said - "It is finished."

On the morning of March 11, 2011 I heard, "Tell them."

- The King is coming.
- This is the End Time.
- You must choose now - God or Not God.

And so I have.

ABOUT THE AUTHOR

Christian writer, Lynn Baber, shares with readers her wealth of experience and a passionate love of Jesus Christ and the principles of worthy leadership and right relationship.

A business consultant, motivational speaker, and one-time political candidate, Lynn exchanged the board room for the barn at the end of the 1980's. Her success as an equine professional includes achievement as a World and National Champion horse breeder and trainer, judge, Certified Appraiser, and expert witness.

Lynn says the messages she delivered as a motivational speaker were absolutely correct; the difference today is that she knows where they may be found in the Bible. Every gospel message is true and the most worthy leader is Jesus Christ.

An author, blogger, and director of Amazing Grays Ministry, Lynn is blessed to live in the barn with her husband, horses, and dogs in Weatherford, Texas.

OTHER TITLES BY LYNN BABER:

Amazing Grays, Amazing Grace: Pursuing right relationship with God, horses, and one another (2010)

He Came Looking for Me: A true story of hope and redemption (2011)

The Art of Being Foolish Proof: The best kept customer service secret (1989)

CONTACT INFORMATION

Lynn Baber
www.LynnBaber.net
lynn@LynnBaber.net

Amazing Grays Ministry
PO Box 187
Weatherford, TX 76086
www.AmazingGraysMinistry.com

Published by Ark Press 2012